The
Book
of the
Poor

The
Book
of the
Poor

WHO THEY ARE, WHAT THEY SAY,

AND HOW TO END THEIR POVERTY

Kenan Heise

Marion Street Press

Portland, Oregon

Published by Marion Street Press
4207 SE Woodstock Blvd # 168
Portland, OR 97206-6267
USA
http://www.marionstreetpress.com/

Orders and review copies: (800) 888-4741

Printed in the United States of America
ISBN 978-1-936863-33-4

Library of Congress Cataloging-in-Publication Data pending

Contents

FOREWORD

A homeless man, who—in composing this—has chosen to share with the reader the plight of his friends, a family of "really nice people."

I hope people will read this book and come to know what's going on.

Friends of mine lived in the Uptown neighborhood of Chicago. They are really nice people. They've got two kids, but they use candles—lots of them—because they cannot afford electricity. They haven't had any other lights in a long time.

I worry about it because of the children.

Several years ago, six small children living in Chicago just north of them died in a fire caused by candles. Several months earlier their electricity had been shut off and their parents were forced to use candles to light the apartment.

My friends told me the kids are used to burning candles and are careful, but I find it awfully scary.

The family couldn't use their refrigerator either. They traded the groceries they could buy with their Link Card for cash and used the money to pay the rent.

To get food, they mainly dumpster dived.

Nothing, nothing at all, is easy for them.

Now, they are gone. I do not know where or why. I've asked neighbors and they didn't know either.

I know how it is. I was married and we had a kid. We never had enough food and we had to move often.

Cornelius M.

ACKNOWLEDGMENTS

I owe my deepest appreciation to the many individuals who offered hands, voices, comments, suggestions, corrections, encouragement, or support in producing this book.

The process of compiling it has been a joint venture of those persons living in poverty whose voices animate the book as well as so many people and organizations truly and energetically fighting poverty in our country and around the world.

Together, they tell—in a new language—the story of poverty. The book speaks specifics rather than generalizations, facts rather than conjectures and, more than anything else, about people and their lives.

Throughout *The Book of the Poor*, you will find hundreds of examples of this language along with a compelling narrative as we hear of

- a man in a store surreptitiously stuffing pigs' ears and a beef tongue in his pocket and then begging a quarter from someone who had seen him do it,
- a woman who prays for those who help her and for those who don't want to,
- a mother on welfare who tells us "whatya cuts down on first" when the money stops coming in,
- real people and organizations all across this country determined to cut poverty in half within ten years or simply to end it, and
- 173,045,325 people around the world who have made a commitment to stand up against poverty.

I especially want to acknowledge those involved with the many organizations mentioned throughout the book. Their extraordinary generosity in behalf of this venture encourages me to say that any reader who contacts them in an effort to be of use will meet with a similar welcome.

The quality, even the adequacy of the writing and editing of the book, is due in enormous measure to the diligent efforts of my wife, Carol, and my brother, Joris. They had my back every page of the way. Help also came from Chris Thale, Tami Peden, and Bob Ford.

A special thanks goes to Marion Street Press and its owners, Jim Schuette and Kel Winter, who maintained a highly personal interest in the process and who have contributed the meaningful support every writer craves.

I also want to thank the *Chicago Tribune*, which time and again over the years afforded me the opportunity and encouragement to interview the poor and destitute and give them a chance to speak for themselves.

I have found Deborah Weinstein and the Coalition on Human Needs, of which she is the executive director, to be at the core of what is organizationally being done on behalf of the needs of the poor. She opened crucial doors in reaching others who are leading the fight against poverty throughout the country. In doing this, she contributed immeasurably to the helpful material you will encounter in the following pages.

I would like to acknowledge the support and generosity of Michael Katz and Robert Reich in allowing us to quote their material in a number of places throughout the book.

Finally, a special thanks to PolicyLink and to Spotlight on Poverty: The Source for News, Ideas and Action, an initiative managed by Center for Law and Social Policy (CLASP). The articles they have permitted us to reprint are simply superb in significance, content, and style.

I offer ahead of time a deep-felt gratitude to those who will embrace this work and help it to reach others.

INTRODUCTION

Deep within each of us burns a spark—acknowledged or not—that reminds us that poverty is a manifestly intolerable affront to humanity. Call it conscience or an awareness of our shared unalienable rights, but it tells us that:

- Poverty is hunger,
- Poverty is lack of shelter,
- Poverty is being sick and not able to see a doctor,
- Poverty is not knowing how to read,
- Poverty is not having a job,
- Poverty is fear for the future,
- Poverty is living one day at a time,
- Poverty is powerlessness,
- Poverty is lack of representation,
- Poverty is lack of freedom,
- Poverty is a situation people want to escape,
- Poverty is a call to action.

Though not a definition, this description begins to say what being poor means. It is borrowed from the website of A Minnesota Without Poverty (www.mnwithoutpoverty.org), one of the multitude of organizations across our nation bonding together to eliminate it.

Despite our inner spark, our consciences, and the shared rights on which this nation was founded, a counterforce seems to be building almost day by day. It is a disdain for the poor that, like a dark cloud, hovers over them. Its shadow and its demeaning threat hurt the most vulnerable of our fellow Americans.

The challenge is to eradicate the disdain against the poor, help them to meet their basic needs, and restore their role in our society as producers and consumers—in other words, to end poverty.

Those who are picking up weapons to fight poverty and disperse the disdain associated with it are fast becoming a visible army across this nation and throughout the world.

In the upper right-hand corner of the cover of this book is a symbol of this worldwide effort against poverty. The rays of the sun symbolize that the people of the world willing to "Stand Up, Take Action, End Poverty Now." Around the world, 173,045,325 people made such a commitment in 2009. They physically and morally stood up at 3,000 events in 120 countries to pledge themselves to work toward United Nations-formulated Millennium Development Goals to end poverty.

The Stand Against Poverty website (standagainstpoverty.org), which unites people around the world fighting for these goals, reported the breakdown of the *Guinness Book of Records*-verified numbers of people who took the pledge:

> In Asia more than 100 million people participated (101,106,845); in Africa more than 37 million (37,848,412); in the Arab region more than 31 million (31,394,459); in Europe more than 2 million (2,102,121); in Latin America more than 200,000 (229,371); in North America nearly 200,000.

Over the last 50 years, as a newspaper reporter and an author, I have had the opportunity to interview hundreds of poor and destitute people across this country and allow their voices to be heard. In the pages of this book, I have replicated many of these interviews. Some of these have appeared in my books, *They Speak for Themselves: Interviews with the Destitute of Chicago* (YCW, 1965) and *The Death of Christmas*, (Follette, 1971). Other interviews appeared in newspapers for which I worked (principally, *Chicago's American* and the *Chicago Tribune*). Still others are current and have not been printed anywhere before.

In some instances, and with the individual's permission, I have shared the name of a person whom I interviewed. Other times, acting out of respect for individuals' wishes, I have not.

What they need, they have told me, is a slice of the loaf and the right to earn it. What they often ask for first and foremost, however, are respect and recognition of their humanity instead of the disdain with which they are so often met.

A Chicago man on disability told me in an interview:

> I want to express myself for myself and for the other poor devils like me, 'cuz they're existing like I am.

> When you go up to the big people, they think everybody on welfare is the same. They think they're lazy and haven't got the capability to work. You find nine people that are lazy and don't believe in decency and 900 that are trying.
>
> But they put people in brackets. If you're on public aid, you're in the lowest bracket. If you are on disability like I am, they got a different story. They say, "My grandfather was sicker than he is, and he worked."
>
> They say, "When I was poor I lived on $1.47 a day."
>
> They forget that it is now this time and that prices for everything have changed. They got no feeling for poor devils.

A woman in Cook County Jail protested in words that also spoke for many others:

> This society is as anti-black as it is anti-woman. The only way women are going to have sufficient means with which to live after their husbands or baby-makers are gone is to prostitute and steal. After looking for a job for three years and not finding one, I had to figure what to do that was not illegal. There are many people who are angry with us, and they are ignorant. They have no understanding of what we are going through and of what our lives are like.

Another woman added: "They never hear about the mother who is trying so hard she is neurotic and depressed and don't know what she's gonna do."

An urban anthropologist and a respected authority on poverty, hunger, and homeless in New York City, Anna Lou Dehavenon, became as deeply involved as she was, according to her *New York Times* obituary, because she realized how much she had in common with the women in homeless shelters.

As Americans, we say we want and need to integrate the poor into our society; but first we must want and need to hear their voices, tender them respect, and see them not so much as *strangers* but rather as *neighbors*, who have needs and inalienable rights as valid as ours.

In his book *The Undeserving Poor* (Pantheon, 1989), Katz takes our nation to the next step: "Mainstream discourse about poverty, whether liberal or conservative, largely stays silent about politics, power, and equality. But poverty, after all, is about distribution; it results because some people receive a great deal less than others."

What Katz is saying can be summed up in two words: unequal and unfair.

The words of the poor and the destitute throughout this book let them say what they want and need.

In the following pages, you will encounter people who dumpster dive for food and often share what they get with others who need the food. You will hear a homeless man describes what it means "to sleep under the viaduct," and you will hear how boys who live on the streets make a living the only way they know how.

You will learn about a poor woman in Philadelphia who has found a way to speak for herself: she took a photo of the small amount of coins she had to count on to survive, and that picture became a part of an exhibit on poverty in the Rotunda of the United States Capitol.

A number of Florida residents with serious medical problems will share with you their worries about cuts in Medicaid and the harm these could bring into their lives.

You will visit jail and very poor neighborhoods; you will stop to hear the stories of panhandlers on Chicago's bridges and street corners.

Your journey will climax in interviews with people representing large organizations who are working together to fight poverty in the United States and throughout the world. These interviews will include personalized invitations by these individuals and their organizations to fight the battle with them.

You will find both need and hope in these pages. More importantly, you will learn of progress which you can supplement.

Section 1

THE POOR, YOU, AND I

Poverty is the moral and spiritual issue of our time.
—Tavis Smiley

Are You Poor?

While Thomas Jefferson was in France in 1785,
he wrote the following in a letter to James Madison:

As soon as I had got clear of the town I fell in with a poor woman walking at the same route with myself and going the same course. Wishing to know the condition of the labouring poor I entered into conversation with her, which I began by enquiries for the path which would lead me into the mountains: and thence proceeded to enquiries into her vocation, condition and circumstance. She told me she was a day labourer, at 8. sous or 4 d. sterling the day; that she had two children to maintain, and to pay a rent of 30 livres for her house (which would consume the hire of 75 days), that often she could get no emploiment, and of course was without bread. As we had walked together near a mile and she had so far served me as a guide, I gave her, on parting, 24 sous. She burst into tears of a gratitude which I could perceive was unfeigned, because she was unable to utter a word. She had probably never before received so great an aid. This little attendrissement, with the solitude of my walk led me into a train of reflections on that unequal division of property which occasions the numberless instances of wretchedness which I had observed and is to be observed all over Europe.

I had an encounter of my own some 226 years later.

"Are you poor?" I asked the woman sitting next to me on a bench as we waited for public transportation.

Nothing in her appearance or demeanor indicated that she was poor or was not. My question would seem to be a social no-no. Many people forced by their circumstances to answer yes would tend to consider it a matter of shame to be poor. How dare I, then, take a chance of embarrassing her by making such an inquiry?

Her straightforward glance, however, had given me a certain boldness to raise the question. It had encouraged me to believe she would find my question respectful rather than intrusive.

We had been talking for several minutes. In our conversation, the subject of poverty had arisen and she had demonstrated a marked sympathy for people in want. As a result, I felt the freedom to ask what I did. Other discussions over the years have taught me that, if people feel they can trust you, they are more than willing to throw off the invisible cloak of being down and out and speak about their lives on a personal basis.

Hesitantly, she answered, "Yes."

Then, even more openly, she continued,

> Saying we are poor is a reality check for me. I have three small children and my husband is young. The only work he can find is moving furniture. It pays very little and he barely makes enough to meet the rent.
>
> We have to rely on the government for help in putting food on the table and getting any of the health care my children need.

Hesitating for a second, she added "There is much we need that we do not have. Still, so many are lots poorer than we are; but, yes, I am—we are—poor."

A frustrating sadness edged her words; but I heard no complaining, no "feel sorry for me" message in them.

She got up, smiled, boarded the vehicle and went away.

A homeless friend, with whom I discussed this conversation and who called himself "very poor," commented:

> A lot of us try to hide that we are poor. I don't know the real reason why we do. I try to look my very best so people won't know and won't feel sorry for me. I don't want people to feel sorry for me. That is the way most of us are.
>
> As a result, people don't begin to know how many of us there are. My teenage son was living with my ex-wife, his mother. I rarely went to see him because I did not want him to know I was living on the streets.
>
> Finally, I decided he was old enough and I should tell him the truth. His mother agreed.
>
> He was deeply relieved.
>
> "I always thought it was because you didn't love me," he said.
>
> He then took me around and introduced me to all of his friends.

The similarities in the encounters that Thomas Jefferson and I had can say much about poverty, what it is and what we can do about it.

First and foremost, poverty is personal and grinds people down like waves against rocks. Those two women—226 years apart—exemplified this wearing down course in those details of their lives, which they elected to share. And, unbelievably, there is a historical connection between the two women.

It is a constitutionally affirmed obligation of the United States government to deal with poverty and destitution and to raise taxes to do so under its responsibility "to promote the general welfare." That is what the courts have said and men and women in the military over the years have died for.

The woman whom Jefferson met on the path was representative of a significant group of people in history—the desperately poor women of France, who would out of their desperation four years later help initiate the French Revolution.

The one who opened up to Jefferson about her desperate financial need was of the same material as the wick that was lit and caused France to explode in the 1780s. The political rebellion was not first against the ages-old French monarchy, which believed it had a divine right to rule, but so that peasants would not starve.

She conceivably could have been one of the women in the Paris marketplaces on October 5, 1789, who broke out in a near-riot over their poverty and the high price and scarcity of bread.

They felt angry and trapped. The storming of the Bastille prison had been four months earlier and had inspired in them an incipient sense of rebellion. Then, joined by other protestors, the women marched on the city armory, ransacked it for weapons and continued onto to the royal palace at Versailles 20 kilometers away. The crowd—which had grown into the thousands by then—was able to compel the king, his family, and the entire French Assembly to return from Versailles to Paris. In doing so, the crowd had demystified, if not all but dethroned, the king.

Jefferson was then the American ambassador to France. He was, at this point, strongly supportive of the direction in which events were going in France. He left the country, shortly after the historical Women's March on Versailles to serve under George Washington as America's first Secretary of State.

In meeting the woman on the path, Jefferson was encountering one of the ten million underpaid, underfed, or starving peasants in France.

As he wrote the letter, he and James Madison were engaged in a correspondence on how much the Articles of Confederation, which governed the newly formed union of the American states, needed to be changed. The poverty of the woman helped throw in a new quotient. The issues that fomented the French Revolution were far more associated with poverty and the immediate needs of the poor, than were the core issues that created the American Revolution. The drafters of the United States Constitution would have to address human need, in whatever document they generated to form a more perfect union.

It was in this context that Madison would add a highly significant phrase, "the general welfare," first to a revision of his home state's constitution called "The Virginia Plan," then to the United States Constitution, and finally to a section of the document that gave the new government the right to tax citizens. The phrase—deliberately or not—cemented the people's needs to the purview of American government.

In an 1831 letter written in his old age, Madison raised some question about limiting the intentions of the phrase, but the Articles of Confederation, the Virginia Plan, and the United States Constitution all contained those words and the Constitution specifically listed it as a justification for raising taxes.

Whatever his intentions might have been then, Madison's very deliberate phrase had opened the door to the government of the United States accepting the responsibility inherent in the words of the Declaration of Independence, "created equal" and "the unalienable rights of life, liberty, and the pursuit of happiness."

Those two women who spoke of their lives—226 years apart—stand like sentinel interpreters of the theme in this book: What the poor want and need is a slice of the bread of abundance, and their right to earn it. The two both acknowledged to the interviewer that they were poor. Their words approach us, however, not with beggars' cups or sad tales, but as neighbors illuminating the truth about poverty and why we need to mitigate and, if possible, end it.

We do not choose to riot, break into an armory and take up guns, nor haul off out of their castles those who own the wealth. There are, fortunately, other ways we can select.

This generation has created a new sense of protest and indignity over the very issues, which were ripe in the 1780s. And those who seek to occupy Wall Street and other power places in this nation have made it clear the issue concerns the general welfare and the need and responsibility of We the People and the government we founded to maintain it.

As a journalist since 1958, I have interviewed hundreds living in poverty in America. I published them in two books and four newspapers. One the most memorable interviews was with an African-American woman on the West Side of Chicago. She called herself "Big Mama," referring—I believe—to her role in her household and neighborhood as well as her weight. I had asked her the question, "How do you survive when there is no money coming in?"

She spoke in a voice that she later acknowledged as "speakin' Southern":

> Don't ask me how you survive when the money stops coming in. That's what I wants to know. But I'll tell ya what ya cuts down on first.
>
> The first things peoples can cuts down on are gas and lights. Ya puts more clothes on. I even saved $5 one month by burning an oil lamp.
>
> But ya really have to have one 40-watt bulb in the house to see and read by. The rest can be 25-watt light bulbs. And it's a sin to burn a light during the day. I went in one house and theys had a 75-watt bulb and theys even had to use a shade.
>
> And ya can turn yer refrigerator off at night if ya ain't got any perishable meats in it.
>
> We uses gas and that's expensive. But the gas company is good. They shuts off the gas and I goes downstairs and turns it back on. They knows me.
>
> I hear that one onion is worth a whole plate of anything else. So we cuts up an onion and puts it over rice or potatoes. Or ya can cut out the vegetable if ya got canned fruit. They counts the same.
>
> Mainly, we fill 'em up on potatoes or rice or spaghetti or corn bread. You don't feeds 'em potatoes or corn bread at the same meal like some people I know. And the rich people has salads and vegetables at the same meals. That ain't necessary for nobody.
>
> Ain't none of these kids right now got any underwear. I can get an undershirt for 20 cents at Goodwill.
>
> A woman's dress is the best thing to buy for a child or a lil girl cuz it's got the best materials in it. All you got to do is cut it down and ya got a real good dress.
>
> You can get by, but you can't survive.
>
> For entertainment we all goes to church.

2

Poverty in the Lives of Three Women

The big (poverty) numbers muscle out an important back story: with-
out government programs, poverty levels would be even worse.
—JODIE LEVIN-EPSTEIN, DEPUTY DIRECTOR OF
THE CENTER FOR LAW AND PUBLIC POLICY

The three women whose interviews create the framework of the prior chapter tell us much about what being poor means.

The first, the woman in France, was poor and the only help we see her getting was occasioned by an accidental meeting in 1785 with a future president of the United States. We speculate about her being in a parallel situation with the women whose desperation four years later ignited the bloody French Revolution.

The second is a woman of today, able to get by and live with her poverty because government programs help supplement her husband's low wages. Her family needs more and the right to earn it. She wants not to be poor. In the meantime, she is short of being desperate, but only because her country has come to her family's assistance.

The third is a woman who was interviewed in 1964 and has had to cut down on everything on her table and in her house for her children to survive. The interview with her was before the War on Poverty programs and food stamps that changed the lives of individuals such as she. She was more like the French peasant woman than the poor woman today.

In the next five years after my interview with her (1965 to 1969), the War on Poverty would help lift 12 million Americans out of the kind of poverty that she and her children were experiencing.

What if those millions of the poor had not had their lives improved? What might have happened to their children beyond whatever did? Would the economy have stalled? Would our nation and their world have become even more dysfunctional? Would something comparable to the Women's March on Versailles have occurred? Would there have been a French Revolution-type uprising?

What did happen is that poverty was sliced almost in half by 1972 and the desperation of many cut by more than that. Poverty has continued to grow over the last five decades, receiving a jolt from cuts in services for the needy during the Reagan administration.

The aid that came under the stimulus programs included the Supplemental Nutrition Assistance Program (SNAP), the food stamp program that now helps put more and healthier food on the table for millions of people each month.

Jodie Levin-Epstein shows us the powerful and helpful effects of government programs in the lives of the poor in the following article that appeared on The Huffington Post September 13, 2011. She is the deputy director of Spotlight on Poverty and Opportunity and writes for www.clasp.org.

Poverty Reduction: The Invisible Hand of Government

The big numbers (in the United States Census Bureau's 2011 report of the number of people living below the poverty threshold) muscle out an important backstory: without government programs, poverty levels would be even worse.

In part, this tale has not made it to center stage because it's easier to talk about how many people are living in poverty but far more difficult to draw attention to how much worse it would be without interventions. Another reason is that there are political forces dedicated to dismissing the role of government so that they can shrink it and "drown it in the bathtub." Even if that means, for example, that more people will fall into poverty.

To count as poor in 2010, annual pre-tax income for a family of four must have been below $22,314, which translates into $107.00 per person per week. The Census data reveal that in 2010:

- The poor are getting poorer with nearly half (44 percent) living in extreme poverty, which is less than half of the threshold. This translates into about $11,000 per year for a family of four, or $53 per person per week. The 20.5 million who live in extreme poverty is the highest ever recorded. Their numbers are greater than Florida's entire population.
- Full-time workers too often are among the poor including 2.6 million who work full-year. Their numbers are equivalent to Nevada's entire population.

- Too many children are poor with those under age 18 making up more than one-third (35.5 percent) of those living in poverty even though they are only 24.4 percent of the total population.
- Elder poverty has not disappeared with one of every 11 seniors living in poverty.

As much as poverty has grown, it would have been worse without government playing a role. More than 4.5 million people stayed out of poverty during the Great Recession thanks to seven provisions in the American Recovery and Reinvestment Act, according to a Center on Budget and Policy Priorities report, which used an improved poverty measure to assess the impact. In New York City, the Center for Economic Opportunity found that government programs and policies reduced poverty by 3 percentage points between 2008 and 2009. An analysis in three states by the Urban Institute found that child poverty was cut in half due to safety net programs.

The Census report provides a peek at government programs' anti-poverty effects. For example, if tax credits were counted, the value of the federal earned income tax credit would reduce the number of children classified as poor by 3 million. In 2010 poverty was also reduced by:

- 3.2 million people through Unemployment Insurance
- 20 million people including 14 million elders aged 65 and over through Social Security

While the success of government safety net programs should be celebrated and protected, they are necessary but not sufficient. Government investment in decent jobs is an important piece of making the invisible hand of the market work well for low-wage workers, particularly now, in the aftermath of the Great Recession and with a sticky 8-plus percent unemployment rate.

The nation needs jobs and the poor need jobs with livable wages. Three decades of wage stagnation have chipped away at the middle class and are now hitting low-wage workers hardest. Notably, median earnings for male workers with a high school diploma fell by over one-third between 1969 and 2009.

The administration's American Jobs Act offers valuable strategies. In addition to proposals that provide incentives to hire the long-term unemployed and use unemployment insurance to expand work-share programs that avoid layoffs, the jobs package establishes a Pathways Back to Work Fund aimed at investing in low-income youth and adults. Pathways includes funds for a proven wage subsidy program, jobs for youth, and work-based training initiatives.

These and other worthy notions face more than the usual political challenges. Instead of leaders dueling over how best to provide opportunity and protect vulnerable families, some political forces promote policies that would reduce the incomes of already low-income families. One notion being floated is that low-wage earners, including the 7 percent of workers who live below poverty, should pay more taxes. More than one conservative presidential hopeful is calling for a hike in these workers' federal income tax. Charges that such actions are unsound, even immoral, are inevitable. But another conservative notion, that most of the poor are "allegedly" poor and not "truly" poor, will likely be used by these political figures to deflect the charge of immorality. After all, if most of the poor are only "allegedly" poor, where's the harm? Politicians cloaked in the belief that most of the poor exist only "allegedly" risk behaving indifferently to those who get by on little income. That's a moral hazard the nation can ill afford.

The public, it turns out, wants more government attention to poverty reduction. One recent poll found that 56 percent believe that the government does not give poor people enough attention. Another poll found that 64 percent want more federal government involvement in reducing poverty.

It's time to hand it to the government. Its programs can make a visible difference.*

---

* Reprinted with permission from Jodie Levin-Epstein, "Poverty Reduction: The Invisible Hand of Government," The Huffington Post, 13 Sept. 2011.

3

Hurricane Katrina and the Really, Really Poor

"But, still no one came."

O nce in a while, most of us—though not very often—get an introduction to the poorest of the poor. When it does happen, they become visible and so does their abject suffering. And then we know they exist and, for many people, a spark of caring turns into a fired-up conscience anxious to do something.

We saw the poor and those without recourse alive, real, and suffering in the wake of Hurricane Katrina that hit New Orleans and the Gulf Coast in August 2005, ripping aside the curtain concealing America's deep but well-hidden poverty. Without transportation or a place to go, many poor and resourceless people in New Orleans and along the Gulf Coast were caught up in a shocking tragedy that will be recounted for centuries.

Government officials in charge had neither the will nor adequate plans to evacuate those who became stranded or were herded into the Superdome and became trapped there for days. Whatever excuses were made, the real problem seemed to be that the planners and rescuers did not see the poor as people deserving of an all-out effort.

These were people without cars, without phones, or other means to get reports of what was happening or going to happen. They were people without provisions for today, much less tomorrow. The entrapment of Katrina's impoverished victims was a metaphor for what happens daily to people, but on whom we focus neither TV cameras nor our eyes. In New Orleans, the stunning reality was there for us to see.

The levees had broken, the water had risen, and the helpless residents had climbed to their roofs to survive.

Minutes went by.

They were frightened near to death.

Hours passed.

The water rose higher. They thought they would drown or die of the heat unless someone came soon.

Afternoon turned into evening. It grew dark.

The dogs howled all night.

There was no drinking water. No food. No medicine. The children cried and did not stop crying.

The next day came.

The heat, even of the morning, was unbearable.

The hunger and thirst were worse.

Morning turned to afternoon.

Fear turned into terror.

Night came.

No one slept, or did so only for a few minutes at a time.

Morning arrived. Someone had disappeared in the night.

The sun grew hotter; the smell, ever more nauseous.

What was happening to their neighbors, to their families, to their friends? What was going to happen to them and how soon?

Evening arrived. A body floated by and then another.

The crying wore out. It was replaced with sadness piled on top of fear.

The next day came and the day after came.

The heat churned the flooded streets into fetid sewers. Planes and helicopters flew over with camera crews, the military, and politicians; but no amount of arm waving or yelling produced any results.

People died, dear family members and neighbors, but still no one came.

The television just weeks before had shown American naval vessels scrambling across the ocean to save Russians trapped in a submarine.

But for ever so long no one reached the flooded neighborhoods of New Orleans. No one came to rescue the children, the pregnant women, the grandparents, the dying, for four days, for five days and for some, seven or even ten days.

Why?

Because even though we watched, saw the pictures and heard the cries, the voices and the tragedies of New Orleans' poor on our radios and television screens, somehow even our federal government and its agencies were recalcitrant. There was not that urgency of a comrade left behind on the battlefield.

Perhaps, if the poor, very real people of the city had been included in the pre-Katrina disaster planning, they would have known enough to ask,

"But how is my family, how am I, going to get out?"

If the poor people of New Orleans in need of help on their rooftops had the ear of the president or his advisers, they might have been able to shout into it, "Come with help NOW!"

Dr. Lance Hill is the Executive Director of the Southern Institute for Education and Research, a tolerance education and race relations research center based at Tulane University in New Orleans. It reports that in New Orleans 65 percent of black children under the age of five are now living in poverty.

Writing on the website of the Louisiana Justice Institute, Dr. Hill said:

> With all the triumphal rhetoric of New Orleans as a city rising from the dead, the Census Bureau data offers the harsh truth that some have risen while others have fallen. We act at our own peril if we ignore these troubling developments; the problems of education and youth crime and violence cannot be solved as long as local blacks are unfairly deprived of the economic benefits of the recovery and the jobs for rebuilding the city.

4

The Cause of Death—Poverty

Deaths from the factors of poverty in this country are devastating, routine, unacceptable, unfair, and painfully real.

When an adult or child dies because of falling through the safety net, the cause of death has rarely been listed as "poverty." Yet, that is exactly what belongs on millions of death certificates throughout the world. It would be a sad word in a tragic place.

Deaths from the factors of poverty in this country are devastating, routine, unacceptable, unfair, and painfully real. The poignant fact is not in the numbers, however, but in the child, parent, brother, sister, relative, or friend taken for one of the most inexcusable of reasons—individual poverty or destitution.

The wail about the loss of relative or friend from such a cause should sear through the consciences of all. I mumble a litany of names as I recall those whom I have known who died from such a cause. Medical investigators in *The American Journal of Public Health* (2011) reported that

> ... approximately 245,000 deaths in the United States in the year 2000 were attributable to low levels of education, 176,000 to racial segregation, 162,000 to low social support, 133,000 to individual-level poverty, 119,000 to income inequality, and 39,000 to area-level poverty.

While these figures represent approximations and generalities, experience is even more formidable evidence of the cause of shortened life among the very poor. The above figures do not tweak out deaths by lack of medical care, poor nutrition, violence, inherited diseases, poor water supplies, poverty-related obesity, dangerous working conditions, unsafe means of transportation, distance to hospitals, fires, heat or cold, unsafe house and apartments, living on the streets, and even starvation. These are not hypotheticals. They are common causes of death among the very poor, but rare among those who are better off.

The Prevention Institute has published a *Trajectory of Health Disparities*. It outlines the following elements that contribute to health factors with life and death health consequences:

- Individuals are born into a society that neither treats people nor distributes opportunity equally (*root factors*).
- These root factors, such as discrimination, poverty, and other forms of oppression, play out at the community level, affecting the overall community environment (*environmental factors*).
- People affected by health disparities more frequently live in environments with
  - toxic contamination and greater exposure to viral or microbial agents in the air, water, soil, homes, schools, and parks;
  - inadequate neighborhood access to health-encouraging environments including affordable, nutritious food; places to play and exercise; effective transportation systems; and accurate, relevant health information;
  - violence that limits the ability to move safely within a neighborhood, increases psychological stress, and impedes community development;
  - joblessness, poverty, discrimination, institutional racism, and other stressors;
  - targeted marketing and excessive outlets for unhealthy products including cigarettes, alcohol, and fast food; and
  - community norms that do not support protective health behaviors.
- These kinds of environmental factors in turn shape behaviors (*behavioral factors*), such as eating and activity patterns, tobacco and alcohol use, and violence.
- The combination of environmental and behavioral factors contributes to an increased number of people getting sick and injured and requiring screening, diagnosis, and treatment (*medical services*).
- Inequities in access to and quality of medical services for people of color are well-documented and contribute to even greater disparities in health outcomes.

5

You

I pray for those who help me and I pray for those who don't want to help me. I am a Christian and that is the way.
—A MOTHER ON PUBLIC AID IN CHICAGO FROM *THEY SPEAK FOR THEMSELVES: INTERVIEWS WITH THE DESTITUTE OF CHICAGO*

A much-ignored voice in each of us urges that we find opportunities to be inclusive rather than exclusive, to open our minds and hearts to those in need, and to be the individuals we were born on this earth to become.

It is not finding that voice that accounts for the bottomless emptiness in us, which allows disdain to override respect toward others, especially those whom the world tempts us to see them as beneath us.

Uniquely sensitive writers such as Charles Dickens, Victor Hugo, Washington Irving, Upton Sinclair, Jack London, Fyodor Dostoyevsky, Leo Tolstoy, Gwendolyn Brooks, and Toni Morrison have repeatedly afforded the inspiration.

The opportunity to become more than who we are can be encouraged by such writers, but it also can arise from being exposed to the genuine narrative of the poor themselves. The telling of their story represents more than a window into the details in their lives. Their experiences can teach us respect for sacrifice, patience, resiliency, nobility of spirit, kindness, and hope.

The words of the mother on public aid quoted above certainly represent such a narrative. Her comment shows how bright the spark of dignity can glow in an individual oppressed by poverty.

What is especially extraordinary about such words coming from the poor and the destitute is the stunning contrast they make with the disdain that many people heap on those whom they falsely consider inferior to themselves.

It was as a child in the Depression that I first witnessed the reality of people being down and out, yet holding tight to their humanity. The people were my parents. When there was no money, we still enjoyed the attention and affection they were ready to give. It was there even in my older brothers—still children—who made the effort to share what they did have with those of us who were younger. Then, I began to witness it in other relatives and in neighbors, who helped us feel special when the rest of the world saw only our poverty.

Not everybody. Not always. But it was clear that people were helping others to get by.

I have seen this over the years among the poor and even the destitute. I have witnessed it in mothers, especially those who care for their children's children, when their own children cannot manage, are jailed, sick, or die. I have noted it in the children of the very poor, older brothers and sisters seemly more protective because their world is so much harsher even than mine was.

Not everybody. Not always. But people are helping others get by.

I have observed it often among the homeless, a passing along of useful information and looking out for one another. They can be acutely aware of each other's death diminishing themselves, attending each other's funerals, when or if anyone is able to afford to hold one. And, when there is no service—as is often the case—they tend to speak often and well of the individual as a friend and companion.

I once dressed as a homeless person and traveled with 15 men off skid row on a beat-up old school bus 320 miles from Chicago to Traverse City, Michigan. We had been recruited to be migrant cherry pickers in the orchards there.

One man had been aggressively raucous toward the others on the bus to the point that the crew leader-driver stopped in the middle of nowhere and put him off the bus.

The men did not seem to know him or each other, but I felt in my fear I was the only passenger who did not identify with his plight of having no way to get back to the city.

When we stopped in Benton Harbor, Michigan, for a bathroom stop, two of the men brought out what they had to share with the others. One had used coffee grounds and the other, some hard candy.

Such behavior was what I had least expected. Not always. Not everybody. But the patience and the long suffering are so often there. And so are the sacrifices, the shared hope, the small kindnesses and, as a result, the greatness of spirit.

Even in prison, it can be there—those who have been there tell me. I had a friend in prison who could not write but never had trouble finding someone to write a letter for him or do him a favor. And he in turn helped any number of others. It is the way it is. Not everybody and not always.

There are certainly poor people who are mean, angry, bitter, and self-ish. But poverty in itself does not always bring these traits to the fore. At times, it actually seems to subdue them.

Poverty does sometimes contribute to desperate people committing crimes. But so does wealth, and with far less reason.

I invite you to view the pages of this book as a journey and a chance to meet the people you might not otherwise have—the poor and destitute, who will be speaking for themselves.

All this may not sound true to some, and I respect their experiences as different from mine. Those aggrieved by the action of a poor person do not easily separate out the injustice that might have helped cause the poor their fate.

What obscures the story of the poor, unfortunately, is the miasma of disdain society whips up to hover over them. It seems, at times, to be everywhere a poor person or family is.

This miasma hangs over them, their homes, and their children. It is on their streets, thick in the courtrooms, heavy in public aid offices and workplaces; it is subtle and made out as official in hospitals, schools, and churches. Often it is oppressive among police, caseworkers, store clerks, and nursing home staffs; ever present in lines and all too common on buses; blatant in Congress and state legislatures; and accepted without question in boardrooms and banks. Not always. Not everyone. But it certainly seems so if you are poor and you want to be treated with respect, with dignity.

Only when society finds ways to dispense with this universal, unacceptable, and unspoken disdain against those who are poor, can we hope to mitigate the oppression they experience.

Unfortunately for the poor, the most hurtful treatment arises often not from the distortions of those who know nothing about them. Rather, it comes from the people in whose hands their welfare has been placed: teachers, caseworkers, politicians, bus drivers, store employees, clerks, landlords and janitors, better-off relatives, and the architects of welfare policies.

Not always. Not everyone. It is not always open hostility. More frequently, it is a pervasive lack of the basic respect and reverence due every individual.

You may see it expressed toward those working people who are considered "the help": janitors, waiters and waitresses, minimum-wage fast-food employees, low-salaried clerks, the elderly poor, those who clean up, the beggar, the mentally ill, and those in relationships between clients and the very public service agencies that are supposed to assist them.

You might see this disdain from children, who have picked it up from their parents and express it toward adults and toward their peers who seem "lower" than them.

Often the relentlessness of this disdain builds up into a major cause for poor people not wanting to be seen as poor.

In 1981 the Reagan administration was in the process of making massive cuts in assistance programs to the poorest of the poor. I wanted to write an article for the *Chicago Tribune* on the impact on those against whom the cuts were aimed. I expected to be able to cull the story from the public testimonies, which the various city-subsidized welfare agencies had given before the Chicago City Council.

Not a word of passion or feeling did I find there. I found no attempt at a positive, real life portrayal of those whose benefits were being cut.

I was forced instead to gather my information from real people, from Chicagoans in want. Some friends brought together a group of 15 of the poorest people in the city's Uptown area for me to interview. I wrote down each word they said and compiled it into an article without any interspaced commentary on my part.

The subsequent article ran a full page and a half in the Perspective section of the *Tribune*. The story was as much the tragic failure of the heads of welfare agencies to be able to portray poor people as real as it was the words of the poor. Their testimony revealed the unsympathetic "stranger" attitude of the nation and those who deal with the poor. Although many people see poor persons as "them," they are in fact "us"—fellow human beings.

The situation has, to some extent, changed. More recent efforts such as Half in Ten and Witnesses to Hunger have made a deliberate effort to include the narrative of the poor along with the stark facts and statistics. Half in Ten has gone about it state by state.

The following is an excerpt from the August 9, 1981 *Tribune* interview with the poor of Uptown in which they bared their humanity and concerns:

"How bad it gets."

Michael: I'll tell you how bad it gets. I been down to where the only thing I had to eat was an ice cube.

Wanda: You can cut down on food, specially the last week of the month. You go in a lot of houses and you don't find any food whatever in the house. I know a man eats popcorn the last week of the month.

Carl: I am an ulcer patient. I know what popcorn can do to you.

Wanda: Rice will fill you up. So will spaghetti. Anything with starch. For meat, you used to be able to serve kidneys and neck bones.

Carl: You know what neck bones cost in this neighborhood. Eighty cents a pound. I went into a store last week to buy chicken backs because I wanted some chicken and rice. They used to give away chicken backs. Now, they sold me these chicken backs for 59 cents a pound.

Wanda: And you pay the poor tax. All the prices are higher around here. The poorer the neighborhood, the higher the prices. If these cuts to people on welfare come, I don't know what.

Carl: People are becoming more concerned than I've ever seen them before.

Wanda: Last winter, I found out about an old couple that was only skin and bones. The woman had broken her hip and didn't even know it. She just knew it hurt. They had malnutrition so badly you wouldn't believe it. First, I went home and rounded up all the food I could. Then, I called the ambulance. They didn't want to come at first because it had just snowed. I insisted. Those people were the skinniest I ever saw in my life.

Kay: I was in a store last week. It was a Mexican store. There was a little old man stuffing pigs' ears and a beef tongue in his pockets. He even talked to me and asked me for a quarter. He knew I had seen him taking those things.

Wanda: You got to believe there are a lot of families around here that had no heat at all last winter. One I know, they got an electric heater and then it burned up. Then they had no heat. The kids all dressed up like Eskimos. Not everybody has even clothes enough for that.

* * *

The voices you will encounter in this book are like those you have just read. They are not self-absorbed, stupid, greedy, selfish, but rather belong to intriguing and kind people overwhelmed by being poor.

Charles Dickens, Upton Sinclair, or John Steinbeck portray both villainy and incredible heroism among the poor. We see a special heroic kindness in quotes such as the following from Steinbeck's *The Grapes of Wrath*:

> They's a time of change, an' when that comes, dyin' is a piece of all dyin', and bearin' is a piece of all bearin', an' bearin' an' dyin' is two pieces of the same thing. An' then things aren't so lonely anymore. An' then a hurt doesn't hurt so bad.

I have promised you, the reader, a passage, a journey, in the coming pages. You will listen to unemployed steelworkers who had come into the union office to get a free handout of cheese, telling how long they had labored in the grueling mills and how they had once hoped it would continue through retirement.

You will meet beautiful, resourceful persons, friendly, kind individuals who are really trying—all who are poor, very poor. Yet, millions of Americans lay blame and deny them human services from mental health to dental care—often with a show of pique, contempt, and disdain. These millions of Americans want to punish even the smallest of children for the supposed sins of their fathers and mothers.

They want to distort the facts in order to take away childcare, health care, and Head Start. They want to strip their schools of funding and their most qualified teachers, instead handing over on a dish whatever is good in their education to the children of the wealthy.

They want to deny the poor—even the most innocent of children—opportunity and a chance in life and then proclaim their own righteousness in doing it. They want to take their fathers and mothers and put them in jail for the crimes that arise more from poverty than dark motivation.

They want to refuse the poor trust and respect based on their color, national origin, or immigrant background. They want to confine them to neighborhoods where a chance in life all but does not exist. And they want to take away their right to vote.

And, when the poor get sick, their enemies want to campaign so they have neither insurance nor an open road to decent medical treatment. Despite America's abundance, the poor will continue to die from one of a long line of causes associated with poverty—violence, obesity, poor water supplies, work-related hazards, as well as a variety of cancer, heart, and lung diseases. Above all, they do not want to climb the hill to their crucifixions carrying the crosses of other people's disdain.

Our goal—one we can share—is to allow the poor to defend themselves, let them effectively scatter the malignant cloud of disdain and promote the respect and opportunity they need and deserve.

To the kind and just people of this world, the most satisfying struggle may be the one against disdain and prejudice, and in behalf of respect.

Section 2

THE POOR SPEAK FOR THEMSELVES: AN ORAL HISTORY

If I was on television, I'd tell them. I'd put things out so the big men could see them. I'd tell them that folks just can't make it the way things is. And you got these folks going around making big money and figuring out how people on welfare should spend their money. I'd tell them to try it and feed the food they're talking about to their kids.
But you can't talk to them. You can't go see them. I think talking face to face, they would understand.

—A MOTHER WHOSE FAMILY WAS ON WELFARE, 1965

6

The Poor and the Destitute

You try to save—everybody does that—but an emergency always comes
up. Then it means food off your table and clothes off their backs.
—A MOTHER ON WELFARE, 1965

The following descriptions of family life on public aid come from two books of interviews that I did in 1965 and in 1971. What families reported about their hopes, struggles, and experiences in the first two tells us what it was like for people living in poverty in the mid-1960s as President Johnson was declaring outright war on poverty.

The first two interviews are from my book *They Speak for Themselves: Interviews with the Destitute of Chicago* (YCW, 1965).

A 77-Year-Old Woman Receiving Public Aid

It's too bad we older people are too old for sit-ins and demonstrations. Old people have to eat well to stay out of the hospital.

Each month I get $50.40 from the government as my husband's army pension. He was gassed in World War I and died in 1928. The welfare was giving me $29 a month to supplement it. Last year, they took $3 off of that. What I don't understand is how they can do that with prices going up and all. I guess it's just one of those things you don't understand.

In June, I'll be 78. I think you should be thankful you lived that long.

My rent is $40 a month. We have five tenants in this flat. The others each have one of the bedrooms. I have the living room because it is cheaper since there aren't any closets. I use the hall closet.

After I have paid the $40, I have $36 to eat and live on for the month. I have diverticulitis. I have to eat six meals a day and there are many foods I have to eat and many I can't.

Every once in a while somebody from the church brings me a chicken and a dollar or two, but I am getting desperate.

I worked for years at a resort in French Lick, Indiana and at Warm

Springs, but it was always like they'd tell me there wasn't enough people working there for me to pay Social Security, so I never got it.

The rent has not gone up in the nine years I've been here, but still I have to do something about it. If I could just have an efficiency apartment in public housing. I applied and got a letter telling me that my registration number is 176,561. How far down the list can you get?

I'm not used to being old. I get tired and out of breath easily, especially climbing those stairs. I have a little heart trouble, and it just seems I'm ailing all the time.

I want to keep active as long as I can, but I think this worrying about things is affecting my memory as bad as old age is.

Thoughts from a Mother Who "Cheated" on Welfare

I tell my kid, "You gonna go through school if you gotta eat out of the garbage pail." But he was gonna drop out of school anyway. He heard that he could go to the YMCA and get work. That was in January when they were going to cut us off relief.

I can't write or read, but my husband was a Baptist preacher before we came up here 23 or 24 years ago. Since he died, I've been trying to raise my kids so they wouldn't be robbers. That means you are going to have a hard time. You got to learn to take it. I ain't seen no easy times.

Last year the Social Security gave me a lump sum for my husband. I get a monthly check from them and I report it, but I didn't know you were supposed to report the lump sum, so they were going to take me off disability.

I spent the lump sum to pay off my debts. For three years, I was sick in bed, but they wouldn't put me on relief. Finally, they put me on disability and my kids on ADC. But we had hard times for those years. My kids went three weeks on bread and water. I borrowed money from people, but I wasn't able to pay it until I received that lump sum.

A businessman I hardly know found out about me getting cut off relief, and I went down and saw him. He told me he had to fight with them to get back on. They agreed they would only take off half my clothing allowance for the coming year. I baked him a cake and I told him anytime his family wants a cake, I'll bake it for him.

I'd be glad to have white people and business people help my kid. He's got to live the right life, and there are people who are willing to drag him down. Let me suffer for the food and clothing, but let my kid get his learning.

I haven't had a pair of new shoes in ten years. I just wear the shoes people give us. My sister saw I needed a table and she said, "I'm gonna suffer along with you and give you a table."

Sure some people waste their welfare money on expensive furniture. But they cut every last one of us for what one does. I stay in my class with the cheapest I can get.

When I get my check, I buy enough canned goods to last me a month. We don't eat much meat. My kid is in the ninth grade and it's hard to do everything his teachers say and the ADC say, because you don't have any money and they sets a time you have to do it.

I don't worry. I just pray to the Lord to find me the way.

The following are from The Death of Christmas *by Kenan Heise and Arthur Allan (Follette, 1971):*

A Very Poor Hispanic Mother

I was sick last Christmas and my husband was out of work. The children only got what my mamma sent them and what the church gave them.

It's tough not to be able to give when you want to. It's better to give than to get, as the saying goes, and it's hard when you can't.

A Mother of Five

My children never get birthday gifts. Then here come all these commercials starting in September. They never tell children how much they cost. The kids think they give them away. I'm sad from when the advertisements start until Christmas is over.

The hardest part in my house is that we were not always on welfare. When I was married, the kids had anything they wanted. Now, when the kids ask you, you tell them you'll try.

I hate Christmas now. I grew up poor and I vowed that my kids would have what I didn't.

I wonder how many other people ever had to get up on Christmas morning and face their kids and not have anything to give them. It's really bad on welfare.

You try to save—everybody does that—but an emergency always comes up. Then it means food off your table and clothes off their backs.

How do you explain to your kids that you can't buy them nothing, especially when they see other kids with bikes or trikes, or when they get older, radios and even a television.

My oldest son is emotionally disturbed, and he wants a poodle for Christmas. He found one and I told him he could keep it if no one claimed it, but the owner was found after two days. He knows only one thing: he wants a poodle. The psychiatrist asked him what's his hobby. He said, "Dogs." But there's no room in my budget for poodles.

A Woman in the Cook County Jail Infirmary

Christmas is just another day to me. I'm in jail; I'm not happy about it. It's just Christmas, that's all. If I had the money, I would be out on bond.

A Teenager

My mother, my brothers and sisters are on welfare. Christmas I always remember as the time when you scrimped.

I remember way back the Salvation Army bringing boxes into our house. At the time, I liked it. Later, it bothered me. Why were these people bringing these things?

Christmas—that's when you can really distinguish the haves from the have-nots.

7

The Children of the Poor

Just because a child's parents are poor or uneducated is no reason to deprive the child of basic human rights to health care, education, proper nutrition.
—MARIAN WRIGHT EDELMAN, FOUNDER,
CHILDREN'S DEFENSE FUND, *PSYCHOLOGY TODAY*, JUNE 1975

As I interviewed parents in economic distress, I learned over and over the great disadvantages they and their children encountered at home, in school, from sickness, in the clothing they had to wear, the food they ate, and the fears and disdain they felt.

In early 1965, I talked with a desperate mother on welfare. She spoke with near tears in her eyes about how hard it was for her to see her children have to do without. At the time, the War on Poverty had just been proposed. Hope was not yet inching higher among the poor and unemployed. Her voice was low; but her passion became clear as she talked.

The following interview first appeared in *They Speak for Themselves: Interviews with the Destitute of Chicago*:

> It's not like you don't know how to manage. It's that you have so many places to put so little money.
>
> I know mine doesn't go up in cigarettes. I don't smoke. But they're looking at it wrong about those who do.
>
> The most important thing is sufficient clothes for the kids. They have to have shoes so they can go to school. They have to get an education, that's for sure.
>
> At times I have to keep them homes three or four days until the check comes so I can buy them some shoes. They hate to miss school. If it's not wet or too cold, they put cardboard in the bottom of their shoes and go to school.
>
> I cook cornbread every day. And we'll have stew or chili or spaghetti. Oxtail makes a cheap stew. Cabbage is cheap, but I have

to have three heads of them. String beans are pretty expensive, but you to have them sometimes for a change-up. At the end of the month, you may cut the vegetables and have rice or white potatoes.

I buy canned milk and powdered milk. They basically have powdered milk and some of the canned milk to mix it with.

The children have to have notebook paper. They always say, "Mama, I have to have notebook paper." That's not included in the budget, but it has to come off the food budget because that's something they have to have.

I had planned on buying them some bedclothes. They don't have sufficient bedclothes. I bought coats for the girls at the resale store last year. They had to have something. The one or two things they had, I nearly washed them to death.

Just because they don't want you to have nothing, you still got to be human.

My children don't go to the movies. They ask about it sometimes.

They go into other children's homes and they see it fixed up better. It makes them feel they are lacking in something. They feel bad and it makes them worry. They don't get toys or clothes, and other children say, "Look at my shoes" or "Look at my toy guns." They just stand there and look at them. Quite naturally, it makes them feel bad.

If you buy something for $5 or $10, you're going to run short before the next check and you are going to take it off food money.

People just don't know. They do all that talk. I really don't have no money.

8

Dumpster Diving

The next time you feel like complaining, remember that your garbage disposal probably eats better than 30 percent of this world.
—ROBERT ORBEN, *READER'S DIGEST*, FEBRUARY 1979

A number of the interviews that I did with homeless people eventually focused on their experiences in "dumpster diving." The poor commonly employ the term to describe scavenging food from the large receptacles behind grocery stores or apartment buildings.

In 2012 Cornelius, an older homeless man who has been living in a suburb north of Chicago, started by telling me of the first time he ever tried dumpster diving.

I did it because I was hungry. I was proud and I did not want anyone to see me doing it. I went through dumpsters behind apartment buildings in Chicago. In the first block, I did not find anything, but in the next one I discovered a large pizza with only half eaten. I took it over to the house of a friend, who heated it up so everybody there had some. I did not tell them where I got it from.

I used to do it to find clothes. You would find a pair of pants or shirt and take it the laundry to clean it. I want decent clothing. I don't want people to know I am poor.

Behind grocery stores, I've gotten polish sausages, hamburger meat, and even steaks. Often, I'd find corn, butter and milk and, recently, cottage cheese. I don't like it, but my friend did, and I gave it to him.

Sometimes, he and I find a lot of food and we take what we can get and share it with others.

I never go to the bottom of the dumpster, but he does. Often, that is where the best stuff is and you have to go there after it, but I still don't.

You find a lot of broken glass in there and you got to be careful.

There is one woman, who is a friend of ours, who just jumps into a dumpster and goes through it like nobody else.

If people want to throw away a television set or something like that, they know a lot of us dumpster dive and they will put it next to a dumpster. If they carefully place the remote on top, then that tells you it works.

We also go through the dumpsters people rent when they are moving and want to throw things away. You'd be surprised what you can find and then sell.

You find DVDs, furniture, jewelry, and other things you can sell. Once, I found a bag of coins in with a box that contained clothing. It only contained nickels, dimes, and quarters, but it was a big bag and the total came to almost $100.

Once you get into one of those dumpsters, you never know what you are going to find.

His friend added: "I keep what I need, and I share the rest with other people. I usually keep any meat."

To get the following account of his dumpster diving in 1965, I interviewed Karl Meyer, a friend and a frequent dumpster diver. "Are there many people in the area in Chicago where you live who do it?" I asked. His answer:

I think there are 100 people in the Cabrini-Green Projects neighborhood who go to grocery store garbage cans for food regularly. I would say 100 at least. A lot of them are really dependent on that food. When they come to the end of their welfare check, and if they dig diligently, they can live it out.

The ones you see are mainly the old people and the more odd types you see walking around with shopping bags. They always have the shopping bags.

The best time is Saturday night just before the store closes for the weekend or the night before a holiday like Christmas. When they have all the special food and can't keep it. However, any time during the day might be good. They throw things out all day. When it gets really cold, there are not as many people hunting for food. We can tell. We get a lot more stuff.

From practically any garbage can in the neighborhood we can always get partial loaves of bread that doesn't get stale real easy.

In the summer, the bottle gangs move in. They try to get a

box of something and peddle it. The irresponsible ones dump the garbage all over the place. Others try to leave the place at least as decent as when they came.

You have to be careful and wear gloves. There are often broken bottles in the cans.

Here is a list some of the things we've gotten at different times:

- 8-ounce bags of shelled walnuts.
- After Halloween, a bushel of Halloween candy.
- Eggs on numerous occasions—as many as three dozen eggs as many as three or four times a day. One or two eggs in a carton break and drip down the carton and they throw them away.
- Once, a bushel of apples in good condition.
- Any kind of boxed commodity in which they slit into it when opening it with a knife—flour and dried eggs for example.
- Any kind of can goods with a label.
- Jelly or syrup from a case in which one bottle broke and dropped down onto others.
- In summer, bushels every day of the outside stalks of celery.
- Fruit—once six lemons in excellent condition.
- Broccoli, bunches of it and often.
- One winter night, a whole bag of onions, slightly frostbitten.

If they put the food in a special place instead of the dumpsters and garbage cans, it would become respectable and everyone would go there. Then, the really destitute wouldn't get it.

9

Sleeping Under the Viaduct

The Son of Man has nowhere to lay his head.
—MATTHEW: 8:20

T.M.'s story, Spring 2012

For four years, I've been homeless and mostly living outside. Finally, finally, I was able to get an SRO (single room occupancy in a multiple tenant building) in Chicago. It was great until I awoke and discovered it was infested with bedbugs and I was covered with their bites.

Nobody should have to sleep outside. I mean that. I think of all the guys who do. It is not something you want to do.

I've done a lot of things to survive. We all do. I've been through a couple of blizzards and some really cold times. And we got wet at times, really wet.

The first day I had no roof to stay under, I walked and walked until two or three o'clock in the morning. Finally, I went in a doorway and up some stairs. I slept next to somebody's apartment and made certain I got up before they came out of it.

I've stayed in a homeless shelter in Chicago, but I ran into too many gangbangers and decided it was too dangerous to keep doing it.

I have ridden the "L" trains all night, but twice my pockets were slit while I was sleeping and I lost my I.D. card. There was never any money in my pockets. I didn't have any. They just probably threw my I.D. in the trash, but I was forced to get a new one. Once someone stole my shoes. That was it.

I moved to a suburb where there was a decent shelter, but it was so crowded that I had to wait six months before I could get a bed. I stayed there for a little while, but they cut the beds back to just 20 and I was out on the street again. You wait and wait for an opening, but sometimes they just give the next bed to someone they want to.

There have been times when someone let me stay with him or her. We have all experienced that, but it doesn't last. And let me tell you, there is nothing like having a place of your own.

We call it sleeping "under the viaduct" because it is so much like that, but it is actually under a loading dock. We are not bothered and, when the weather is right, we feel we have something like a place of our own. There used to be four or five places in this town where you could get away from the worst of the blizzards or the storms. Now, there are only two. Once you start sleeping there, others will respect that it is yours.

We had a place for several months where three of us stayed. We had sleeping bags and lots of blankets. Every morning we got up early and hid them. We never told anyone where we hid them, and we had to make certain no one found out.

On the really cold and stormy nights, we went to bed early. We got into our sleeping bags and wrapped ourselves in every blanket we could. The problem was if you had to get up to take a leak or when you got up in the morning. Some guys and some of the women get drunk because it helps them keep warm. I drink because it helps, but I never get drunk.

One of the guys who had too much to drink one very cold night fell down in the street and froze his toes off.

One church has a warming center that is open from 8 a.m. to 10 a.m. and they feed you coffee and rolls. During the day, when it is cold or raining, you stay in the library if you don't make any disturbance. I use the computer there a lot.

The homeless shelter lets you take a shower and, when it has them, passes out blankets.

In the evening, the various churches take turns providing a meal. And, then, it is back to the viaduct, the dock, or a place in the alley, where you try to sleep.

Recently, we've seen more and more homeless, all kind of ages and backgrounds, younger and older people, six or seven new people every week. One dude is about 18 years old and works at Burger King, but doesn't make enough money to get an apartment. Two young people this week are probably only 16 years old.

Those of us who have been around a while help them out. We tell them where they can get clothes or a meal. Some would probably starve to death if they didn't know where to go.

There's a lot of depression going around. Most homeless people have depression problems. One guy when he goes to find work just can't go into the place. He walks back and forth in front. Who knows what experiences or maybe a bunch of experiences he had in the past when he went for a job. Now, when he gets a lead on a job, somebody's got to with him so he will go in the door.

I used to work at a soup kitchen, so a lot of the homeless come up to me and ask me if they can talk. I listen. That's why I know about their depression.

They're depressed because it's hard to be homeless, especially in the winter. I know a couple of guys who froze to death and another one who hung himself.

Winter can really be tough. My buddy and I had to stay out in a real blizzard last year. We had gone around to all our friends who had apartments to ask if we could stay overnight. Nobody had room for us.

You can ride the "L" [train] if you have the money. If you don't, you can ask someone with a seven-day or a monthly pass to put you through the turnstile, but they can lose the pass if they get caught and you can be arrested.

Besides, riding the L at night can be dangerous. I was on a car in which the passengers were robbed at gunpoint. The gunmen saw I was homeless and didn't bother me. I started to get off at the next stop, but then I saw the robbers were getting off. I sure didn't want to be with them.

One night we were in an open parking garage, in kind of an alcove. The snow blew right up to our faces. We survived because each of us was wrapped in three sleeping bags. Otherwise, we could have frozen to death.

10

Drugs, Alcohol, and the Homeless

*Crack cocaine is a substance that affects the brain chemistry of the
user: causing euphoria, supreme confidence, loss of appetite, insomnia,
alertness, increased energy, a craving for more cocaine, and potential
paranoia (ending after use).*

—WIKIPEDIA

T.M. is in his fifties and has been living on the street, off and on, for a majority of those years.

David Kemp is the program manager for North Side Housing and Supportive Services, a program that administers to the homeless in Chicago's northern suburbs. He has a master's degree in psychology as well as years of training and experience as a certified substance abuse counselor in Santa Monica and Venice, California as well as in Chicago. He knows T.M. well. This conversation took place in the spring of 2012.

T.M.: A number of the homeless people I know have gone on crack cocaine or other drugs as a desperate way to deal with their homelessness, the cold weather, their depression, or all three. It really messes them over. I know. I was one of them. If you want to get back on track, it takes at least 60 days in rehab and a lot of help. I have been lucky. A whole lot of people have helped me, and now I stay away from anywhere where people are using, even my best friends.

David Kemp: Crack and other drugs come with rewards. You have to remember that. Even if for only the few minutes you are high, they take away all the troubles you are facing, make you feel good, and take away your tensions. Also, they afford you a bunch of friends in the people you are using them with. You can't go up to someone and tell him or her they are bad for you.

T.M.: And that they are going to cost you all the money you can get.

David Kemp: Yes, you can't tell them that either. They already know that.

T.M.: But it really does make you spend all your money. One guy I know broke into a bar during the night and stole all the liquor they had. There wasn't any cash, so he just took the liquor. He even went back a second time. He and his girlfriend sold it and spent all the money they got the next day on crack. He is trouble. He is not somebody you want to be around or his trouble will become yours.

David Kemp: People are going to quit when they want to quit. As a counselor I have learned that, but you can help them take the first step.

T.M.: That is true.

David Kemp: We have come to recognize that getting a place is the key toward dealing with many of the difficulties they are going through.

T.M.: Yes, that is what helped me, being able to get away from the people who were using. People who use cocaine just sit around all day. They are good for nothing but sitting there and shooting up or smoking. They go out in the morning and get what money they can to buy it with. They'll do what they have to in order to get it.

David Kemp: Drugs have an enormous downside. They can and do make users paranoid and feel useless, especially if they mix alcohol with cocaine or whatever drug they are taking. Furthermore, the high does not last or they don't even feel it. They're addictive not because they bring pleasure or relief, but because those drugs are addicting. And they do cost you all you have.

T.M.: And then there is rock cocaine versus the raw cocaine you used to encounter.

David Kemp: I don't even hear about raw cocaine any more. The rock cocaine is cheaper.

T.M.: Not in the long run. You gotta have it until all your money is gone. In that way, it is always a lot worse.

David Kemp: We want to get people off of it, but that is not how we approach them. We don't act as though we are police. If we find them an apartment, we don't show up unannounced. The prevailing philosophy used to be that you got them straightened out before you found them an apartment. That approach did not work. This one, we have found, can.

T.M.: Yah, when I had an apartment, no one came and looked through dresser drawers or anything like that.

David Kemp: We find people will open up a lot better if you are not there directly trying to get them to stop using and that it is not a factor in what you are trying to do.

T.M.: I agree. Getting away from others is the only thing that works for me. I think about those guys and the women just sitting there spending their days with their cocaine or beer or reefer or whatever they are using. The only thing they are good at is sitting. I was that way, and I don't want to be anymore. Right now, I'm staying with somebody. My friend came over with a six-pack. I told him to leave it outside the apartment.

David Kemp: We're going to find you a place and a decent one.

11

Reaganomics Put Women in Jail

After 1980, the Reagan administration's policies worsened the situation of poor women. Cuts in income maintenance programs, food stamps, health care, and even the administration's early tax policy all fell heavily on them. (Of course, male poverty has also increased in recent years.) The conjunction of demographic trends, ideology, and politics transformed women's poverty into a major public issue.

Through its attacks on social welfare and affirmative action, the Reagan administration, feminist writers argue, pursued an antifeminist agenda designed to "return society to a former, more explicitly patriarchal mode." ... Kathleen Morgan, for example, argues that women are poor because they are women: "The economic subjugation of women exists within a systematic context of group subjugation. The entirety of social relations as well as the mechanisms of social identification are based on male dominance and the maintenance of female dependence."

—Michael B. Katz, *The Undeserving Poor* (Pantheon Books: New York, 1989)

In the following 1982 group interview with some of Chicago's poorest women, they put to the fire the hand that conceived the Reaganomics' welfare cuts. The five women whom I interviewed were at the time inmates at the Cook County Jail. This appeared in the *Chicago Tribune* as a Neighborhood Dialogue column on February 12, 1982.

Claudia McCormick (supervisor of the women's section of the Cook County Jail): With Reaganomics, people steal to eat. Our current women's population is at 245 to 250, up from approximately 180 a year ago. These are primarily first offenders who are charged with thievery.

The prisoners:

Virginia Gilmore is gray-haired and has a striking carriage.

Jeanette is in her 30s. She asked that her last name not be used.

Debra is nine months pregnant and also asked anonymity. She is in her 20s.

Betty Kelly is a mother in her 30s.

Pat Morris, in her early 20s, is the youngest in the group.

The interviews were conducted in the law library in the women's section of Cook County Jail. The only restriction was that we were not allowed to discuss their legal cases.

Virginia: I believe the word on the streets today is survival. We aren't heartless criminals. We just want to live. We can't even live begging. What we were given in the way of CETA, welfare, and Medicaid are being taken away from us. The core of the people is what Reaganomics is stepping on. I have paid taxes. I have worked all my life. I have given to the Crusade of Mercy.

Jeanette: We don't want to just exist. We want nice things, we want nice homes. We want our children to be educated. We don't want our children to resort to the same tactics we are resorting to in order to survive.

Virginia: People are angry with us because we have to resort to crime. We are angry with them for putting people into office who treat us the way they do, particularly in the court system. If one of them does something, they just get a pat on the hand.

Pat: You can't help but feel real hostile.

Virginia: They're the ones that put the Nixons and Reagans in. We're the poor people. We're the people who make the world work. The upper crust has a voice whenever it needs it. We need a voice to speak for us. You're not here to see when women are crying and to see the women suffer.

Betty: People don't comprehend. My child was hungry. I took him to the A & P, and I took a can opener and a spoon along. I fed him right there in the store. They called the police. They took my child from me and sent me to the 11th and State. You want to know what they did with me? They paroled me to Alcoholics Anonymous because they thought I was drunk.

Jeanette: This society is as anti-black as it anti-woman. The only way women are going to have sufficient means with which to live after their husbands or baby-makers are gone is to prostitute and steal. After looking for a job for three years and not finding one, I had to figure what to do that was not illegal.

Virginia: The population of the women's section of the Cook County Jail hit a record (high) last year. It was even higher than in election years when the alderman sweep the ladies of the night off the streets and the judges try to establish conviction records. That population is going to get higher. We have young first offenders coming in here in increasing numbers. And what for? For thievery. I've been coming to jail regularly for three years, and I haven't seen anything like it.

Jeanette: They are people not having skills, not educated. They were getting welfare, and they cut that out.

Debra: A lot of girls are in here for parole violations. A lot just for not reporting. The jail to me is overcrowded. Some have hard crimes; some don't. Gov. Thompson should make Illinois like Wisconsin. A lot of girls are in here with $50 and $100 bonds they can't pay. In Wisconsin, you can plead no contest right away and be fined. If you can't pay it, you can work it out with an allotment of time served.

Virginia: Once they get us in here off the street, that's all that matters to them. We're not happy with the heat. We're not happy with the food. We're not happy with what's happening on the streets. We're not happy, period.

Jeanette: They're cutting out programs that would give us skills.

Virginia: And without skills, how can we get jobs? One alternative is to take what we need. I am not going to sit by and see my babies hungry and do without. If I have to go to jail for that, I'm going to. There is no justice in our court system.

Betty: Let's say you are just released from prison. The first thing you do is find your family, if you have one. You get done with your laughing and crying and hugging and they try to find a bed for you. Some child has to give up one. So you go to try to get help and you can't. Aid is a long way off. You try to find a job. You can't. So, next night, how do you feel?

Jeanette: There are many people who are angry with us, and they are ignorant. They have no understanding of what we are going through and of what our lives are like.

Virginia: Even though I'm in jail, I still have scruples. I still have character. I have things I wouldn't do.

Debra: I'm nine months pregnant and due any day. I went to court and was picked up on a parole violation on a charge of another felony. I kind of thought I would be picked up when I went to court. When I have the baby, someone from my family will come and pick up the baby. And when someone comes to see me in the penitentiary they can bring the baby along, and I will get to see it.

Virginia: We're intelligent. We're not stupid. I worked all my life. I worked two jobs.

Jeanette: I went to my parole officer and asked for help. He said the best he could do was find me some floor space at Pacific Garden Mission; a cot there. I told him I guess I was just going to have to write me a bad check. He wrote me one himself out of his own pocket so I could get into a public housing project.

Pat: How can you support three kids on $260 a month? People will criticize me for having three kids. Well, three kids are here. Why? They weren't planned. But I now have them and I do love them. If the only way I can prevent their suffering is money and if I need to do something that might bring me in here to get it, I will do it. I can't say I'm sorry. I don't feel that bad I did something, only that I got caught.

Virginia: You know, there are a lot of reasons poor people have kids. There is a need when you are poor to be loved and to feel love, and you turn to your mate for that love and that consolation. You do it when you need it.

Pat: Conditions in this jail are really pathetic. We got bugs and gnats.

Betty: And two girls to a cell.

Virginia: They put us in here like dogs in a kennel. What we get to eat is a soybean substance. On the menu it says meatloaf and gravy. We call it "mystery loaf" or else "murder meat." We get potatoes two times a day.

Betty: And people look at our weight and say, "You must be eating good."

Jeanette: And I want to ask one last thing: Get those racist attitudes out of the courtroom.

Virginia: And those judges who are old and cranky and who discuss our cases ahead of time.

12

The Heart of One of the City's Poorest Neighborhoods

> The children of today are in our hands; whatever we do for them will affect the future. Our lack of faith in this direction is the greatest infidelity. To use a common illustration, a Kentucky farmer will look at a hundred colts and say, "I will train every one of them to become a useful horse." We look at the children and decide that we can save but a few of them; that many must become criminals, many of them a burden on society; that many of them will enhance vice and put barriers in the way of our political institutions. We must believe we can save every child.
> —FRANCIS PARKER, *TALKS ON PEDIGOGICS*, 1894

The following is a *Chicago Tribune* Neighborhood Dialogue column group interview I did November 6, 1981 with mothers living in the Fifth City area of Chicago.

Bordered by 5th Avenue, Jackson Boulevard, and Homan Avenue, it looked like the bomb of poverty has exploded there. The people were poor; the buildings shabby; and city services, such as street cleaning, seemed absent. It was a mostly African-American neighborhood. In the summer, people, rather than have air-conditioning, were hanging out the windows. Representatives of this neighborhood just had to swallow their pride and vote to accept the designation of a slum neighborhood to become eligible for government funds. The vote was not unanimous. Fifth City residents had created a true oasis for their children. It was the Fifth City Preschool Center at 3415 W. 5th Street. Housed in an old factory building, it had 10 clean, but not antiseptic, rooms. The art, made by the children, seemed more creative than one might find in a similar preschool in the suburbs.

Ruth Carter lived two blocks from Fifth City Preschool Center. She had been with the school since 1966 and was its director. Corine Morris, a board member from the beginning, owned a liquor store nearby.

Minnie Wilson was secretary of the school's parent association. Rosemary Melodious helped at the school; she had 10 children and 3 grandchildren. Nola Mae Rose was secretary of the board of directors of the school. Cynthia Johnson and Pamela Underwood each had a child enrolled in the school. Bertha Pinkston owned Fifth Avenue Super Foods and was on the board.

Ruth Carter: In this community, the majority of the families make under $6,500 a year. I know. We discuss income when children want to come to our preschool center. A lot are one-parent families.

Corine Morris: Things around here are tough, a lot tougher than before. So many people are out of work. People who have been working 15 or 20 years are finding their jobs closed. And with what dear old Reagan is doing, it's really tough. People are going down to the unemployment office and standing there for days, only to be told you are not eligible. Come back in 30 days.

Minnie Wilson: They only take so many a day. You have to be down there by eight in the morning when they open. The lines are already formed by then.

Ruth Carter: The cuts have hit our preschool already. We had 65 students at least partially funded through the Illinois Department of Children and Family Services. They've cut it to 40. We survive here in Fifth City. We charge only $25 a week and less when people can't afford that. People volunteer. They volunteer a lot. With that and with donations and contributions, well, we're having problems now with them. We now only have 71 students, but we're licensed for 100.

Rosemary Melodius: We can do without as long as our children have something.

Ruth Carter: We need a preschool here so we can better ourselves and our children can better themselves. Things are getting worse. Our people meet here on Sunday afternoon to see what we really need to do. We grew up together and we're proud of this community. People here volunteer. When we need to come together, we do. They used to call it West Garfield. We call it Fifth City.

Minnie Wilson: They expect us to volunteer. We make $5,000 a year and those who make $50,000 expect us to volunteer four hours a day.

Bertha Pinkston: Police protection is not what it can be. Ladies—especially the elderly—constantly have their purses snatched

Minnie Wilson: I tell people to have some money in their purses. Because if they snatch your purse, then get it in the alley and find nothing in it, you know they are going to come back and get you.

Corine Morris: You call the police and they want to know all about you and about the suspect before they'll come out. You tell them your name and your address and your age and everything, and by then, of course, the suspect is gone.

Nola Mae Rose: People are afraid to go into a currency exchange around here because they know somebody will be waiting for them. But, if you see something going on and call the police, they want to know your name. If you do not tell them everything they won't come out.

Cynthia Johnson: It doesn't make sense. You can't get a police response in the neighborhood without giving your name and all the other information they want. People are scared to do that. And the police commander says we got a communication problem. It doesn't make sense.

Rosemary Melodius: What we got in this neighborhood is a lot of gang violence and little police protection. Our children have to run back and forth to make it to school and back. The Providence-St. Mel's principal and teachers stand on the corners with baseball bats, but it's not enough.

Ruth Carter: It's impossible for our children to learn under these pressures.

Minnie Wilson: I was on a bus last week. A policeman made an arrest. He couldn't get the bus driver to stop. When he did, someone stole the officer's wallet as he was getting off. I told him, and he got it back. He called for a squad car and it took 40 minutes for it to come. I told him, "Now, you know what we go through."

Rosemary Melodius: It's a lot worse now because a lot of the young people had CETA (federally subsidized) jobs. Now they don't have anything to do. It's the worst thing that could have happened when they cut out those CETA jobs.

Cynthia Johnson: I disagree. This gang thing has been stirring up for five years. And that's before they cut CETA.

Rosemary Melodius: It started then and it's been around for years. But it's never been worse. We just don't have enough programs to keep youngsters busy. There's not enough jobs and not enough social programs.

Bertha Pinkston: Then you got the whites, who come into the neighborhood, businessmen in nice cars. When the whites come in the neighborhood it's not only for prostitution. They come here to get other things, narcotics.

Corine Morris: When a shipment of coke comes here, you know it. Everybody does, because you can't buy a roll of aluminum foil for love or money. They use it for packaging the cocaine.

Minnie Wilson: And when it comes to ambulance service in this neighborhood, unless you got a car, forget it. You could walk to any hospital before an ambulance would come to take you there.

Rosemary Melodius: And the hospitals in the neighborhood don't bring me there. If I'm going to die, I'd rather die at home. I don't think the doctors are dedicated to the service of blacks. Take me to County Hospital or St. Luke's. Take me where there is a poor Filipino, who maybe will take care of and feel sorry for me and save my life. That's on the real side. At those other hospitals, I know what they'll do. To them, I'm another nigger.

Minnie Wilson: At County, if you go there, you know you got to pack your lunch and take something to read. You know it's going to take all day, but at least you know they are going to treat you.

Ruth Carter: The problem with the other hospitals is simple: The people who work in them simply do not care about you.

Minnie Wilson: If I had more money, one thing I'd have better is food. Once a month, I try to eat what I want when I want it.

Rosemary Melodius: We do, too.

Ruth Carter: I do, too. You get tired of pinto beans and junk food like potato chips just to keep you full.

Corine Morris: I own Corine's Liquors on the corner. I may have to find some other work or simply go out of business. On any weekend three years ago, we had standing room only. Now, we have what we call sitting room: "Sit anywhere you want." People have this impression that a black man will buy whiskey before he buys bread. Let me tell you, if that were true, my business would not be in trouble. You have alcoholics in any race. They buy cheap. It's the social drinkers who keep my place going. These people aren't buying. In this neighborhood, they haven't been able to keep up with the dime price increases the companies seem to stick on every week.

Ruth Carter: We like to have a drink every once in a while after work. Why not? You can't do that anymore

Corine Morris: It used to be that for $1.25 in this neighborhood you could buy a shot of the best. Now, you give me that and I'll give you a glass of orange juice.

13

Soup Kitchen Meals

It's especially worse for older people. You see a lot of people sleeping in alleys around here. They're in boxes or covered up with cardboard at night.

—TERRIE

Chicago Tribune Neighborhood Dialogue, January 8, 1982

Soup lines had returned to Chicago. Uptown alone had three of them. Catholic Worker movement volunteers staff one at St. Thomas Canterbury Church, 4827 N. Kenmore Ave. every Wednesday and Friday evening at 5:30. They served a meal of rice, beans, and bread and butter, which cost 18 cents per serving. At times the line had 300 people in it. What is life like for people who wait in line up to an hour for this 18-cent meal? This dialogue asked them.

Four persons were huddled in the church doorway an hour before the soup kitchen began serving. Invited to come in from the 20-degree weather, they talked openly of the situations that brought them into line. Carlos gave his last name but when I had difficulty in my repeating the spelling of it, he simply said he preferred that it not be used. The other three—Terrie, Warren, Bill Clement, and John Henry Bell—all lived in Uptown. Bill, however, was looking for an apartment on the South Side. Martin Richey was not in line. He helped out serving the food and ate there as well.

Terrie: I think this soup kitchen is a blessing with rent and groceries as high as they are these days. I have a one-room apartment. I pay $180 a month for it. My social security is $264.70 a month. That leaves $84.70 for everything else. I only come here when I really need to, usually at the end of the month when I get short.

Carlos: I got a complaint, too. I listen to a lot of broadcasts on the radio. There should be more food stamps. You should be able to buy them, especially if you save up money from not buying cigarettes or beer or things like that. President Reagan shouldn't just go after cutting down food stamps. There are more people cheating on income tax.

Bill: Everything's all right with me, only I get robbed every time I'm coming out of the grocery store.

Carlos: I've been ripped off lots of times. The most dangerous time is when it starts to get dark.

Bill: Whenever I come out of the A & P store, I get robbed. When they see you have groceries, they come up and grab you. I've been robbed three times this month. That's why I'm broke today.

John: Christmas is over, and there's no work for me to do. I was ringing a bell for the Salvation Army outside a store, but that's all played out. I made about $100 a week. It was cold. All through December I was out there trying to get people to put money in the kettle.

Martin: They take money out of your pay for you to donate to the Salvation Army when you do that. The pay is $3.80 an hour.

Terrie: Another place people try to kick you out of in this neighborhood is apartments. They just tell you that you can't stay there any longer. And they might take all your clothes if you're behind on rent.

Carlos: They kick you out because they don't like your looks. I've lost deposits of $100 and $140 that way.

Terrie: It's especially worse for older people. You see a lot of people sleeping in alleys around here. They're in boxes or covered up with cardboard at night.

John: And in abandoned buildings. A lot of people sleep in the abandoned buildings.

Terrie: I have it pretty good. I have a roof over my head and, when I have groceries, I even try to help other people.

John: I went to look at an apartment today. The rent was $50. The lady said that it had no heat. You'd have to bring your own heater.

Carlos: You get these small heaters you plug in. They disappear. People come right in your apartment and take them.

John: My daughter has an apartment. She has four small kids. It's a basement apartment and the only heat is a pipe that runs through it and carries heat to other apartments. Beside that she has a small stove that she uses to keep it heated. She has a 5-month-old baby.

Carlos: Second-floor apartments get colder than basement ones. You have to stay in one room.

Terrie: Basement apartments have plenty of cockroaches. My mother's has all kinds of those water bugs.

John: The pane is broken in the bathroom window of my daughter's apartment.

Terrie: Cold apartments are bad for kids. You can cover up tight, but it's bad 'cause they have to go to the bathroom at night.

John: I know a man and a woman lived 13 years on the streets. They said they'd never received any kind of aid, they say they don't give anything. They got food now because of Christmas, they say. After the Christmas food is gone, they don't know what they're going to do.

Carlos: You go to the store to buy some cans of spaghetti, and they rob you. You don't fight 'em. You just hand over your wallet or anything else.

Terrie: You don't go to the currency exchange unless you got somebody with you.

Carlos: Thanksgiving was the best meal I had lately.

John: They feed you real good on holidays. The Jesus people feed real good.

Terrie: At least they give you salt and pepper. The food here is real wholesome. Rice and beans ain't bad. The Salvation Army offers three meals a day on Tuesdays and Thursdays. Other days, it's only breakfast and lunch.

Carlos: Wednesday at 4:30 is the best meal.

John: For breakfast, you get oatmeal. It's dry, and there's no sugar. Sometimes you get powdered milk. You get dry bread, and there's no butter.

Martin: Other meals, it's mostly soup.

John: The ones that work in the kitchen, they eat a little better.

Terrie: And the government is cutting down food stamps.

14

Panhandlers on Chicago's Bridges

What They Had to Say

The following article appeared on the *Chicago Tribune*'s front page under my byline on September 22, 1992.

Paper cups in hand, a small legion of panhandlers cajoles and hectors or silently beseeches passersby on some of the city's busiest streets. On bridges or in front of churches, they stake out a few square feet and sometimes have to defend the territory against would-be interlopers. Some are disabled, some mentally ill. There was a man and a woman with two children. One was a swaddled infant. Many held cardboard signs with scrawled pleas hoping to encourage a passing hand to go into a pocket for a bill or loose change. Some wear hospital bracelets. Few stopped to talk to these men and women. Most pedestrians rushed by, embarrassed or uneasy; some were angered by the constant demands. But if they paused to listen, as this reporter did, this is what they might have heard:

Paul Walton, Randolph Street Bridge

I try to say things to people that are enlightening, like "God bless you, "Have a nice day" or maybe "You have a lovely smile."

People look at you like you're ... an earthworm, a piece of dirt.

You have to keep on going, keep on stepping, swallow your pride. I don't care what one person thinks of me, the next person'll say something else.

This one woman said, "Hey ... get a job." The woman right after her said, "It ain't that easy to get a job," and gave me a handful of change, about two bucks.

Before this, I was a CTA [Chicago Transit Authority] bus driver. I had a problem with alcohol, with drinking, and domestic problems with my wife; I lost it. She went off with somebody. I was married 22 years and had eight kids.

I've been through a hell of a life, and then I will have to turn around and die.

I'm a panhandler. It's a better way of getting money than being out there stealing. I find no reason to carry a pistol.

Maybe I'll get $14 or $15 tops. I try to catch people on payday, Friday. Then, maybe, I'll get $23 or $24.

I'm not a thief, that's one thing for sure. I'm a panhandler, a hustler, call it what you want. I don't like calling it begging.

Larry Bardney, Madison Street Bridge

A man's got to do what a man's got to do. I don't want to steal nothing. I can't get a job. This is my only alternative.

People figure I'm a young guy and I should be able to get a job. I'm 33 years old and am able to work and would like to. Trouble is, there's not any jobs, not for me.

But people are people. Some tell me, "Get a job" or "I'm not going to give you nothing." But there are a lot of people, so I get enough to survive, to eat. Put it this way, I am surviving.

I know it's going to get better. I keep my Bible with me. I know it. That's why I have a smile on my face. I get depressed sometimes. I'm only human.

My last job, I handled toxic wastes, taking drums to a land site. I don't know how dangerous it was, but still I had a job. I was taking a guy's place who had been hurt. When he came back, they laid me off.

I don't understand how a man's going to make it. What do they want you to do, take something or starve to death?

Debbie Kaye, in front of St. Peter's Catholic Church

I live on the streets. I'm homeless.

My health is bad. I need glasses. I have no teeth. I'm 73 years old.

I've tried the shelters. I have a list of them. They give me no security.

Sometimes, I stay by the river.

I've lived in the Loop since I was 18. When I was young, I worked at all kinds of places, Woolworth's—I had four counters there—a dry cleaners, as a waitress, a fry cook, and a dishwasher. I worked for a while in the kitchen at University of Illinois Circle Campus.

I lived down in Miami for a while.

I have a family, but we don't get along. I kind of freaked out. I was married, but I was sued for desertion. Strange habit of taking off.

It's hard. I pray for at least $20 a day.

Mike, Randolph Street Bridge

It's going to get better. It can't get worse.

I started this about a month ago. A friend of mine who stays in the same building I do said it is a way to make some change while you're looking for work.

I have a roof over my head, but everyone in the household is unemployed.

I have an associate's degree in liberal arts. I got it with honors. I had a 3.7 GPA.

There's been different jobs I've had. I worked as a stockboy at Goldblatt's and I've worked pulling up bricks, but the jobs didn't last.

The biggest problem in getting a job is getting your foot in the door. The prospective employers are all looking for someone special. I think everyone's special.

I have been unemployed since last May. I've had a couple of part-time jobs since then.

I know there's a job out there. I do this in the morning. I make a little change. Then, in the afternoon, I put on a tie and the proper suit, get my resumes together and go looking for a job. I put in a full day usually.

A couple of times, I've run into people I knew here. They ask, "What you doing?" and I tell them, "Trying to make a living as best I can."

Jesse Thompson, Madison Street Bridge

I've been doing this for a year and a half. I do it long enough to get me something to eat, and then I go to a shelter.

I'm from Mississippi and I worked on a fish farm there. I came up north because my daughter was in the hospital in Kankakee. She got better, but I stayed.

I can't get a job. I can't read or write so I can't fill out any application. My education is not that good.

People here are not more together like they are where I come from. I don't like it here. Too much violence and prejudice.

I stand here from 6 to 9 in the mornings. I get enough to eat, maybe $10, sometimes maybe $30. Then I go to the park and I walk around.

John Williams, Michigan Avenue

In 1974, I got stabbed with a butcher knife. I lost so much blood I had a stroke.

Around here, everybody knows you and tries to help.

Some call it begging. I call it soliciting.

Police used to give me a hard time, tell me to move on. Now, they leave me alone.

I got a place to stay and I'm on disability. This way, I get enough to eat.

People ask me, "How ya doing?" I tell them, "Pretty good."

Mike, Michigan and Chicago Avenues

Tell people the truth. It's getting worse, a lot worse. People don't have any money to give. They're hardly able to pay the rent and buy food themselves.

It's getting like it was in England years ago. There were only the super-rich and the super-poor then.

Look at these people on the street. You can count the few who have smiles or who look happy. Life is short and people are so miserable.

They're dressed up, but if many of them have more than $5 in their pockets, I'd be surprised. If they stopped credit cards, there would be no tomorrow.

I was a mechanic. I lost everything, family and all. I was just not able to handle it.

I can't get a job. I'm 65. My legs are gone. Thank goodness for the VA hospitals.

I have a place to stay. I get my rent money from this.

What happened? The government in Washington had to have seen this coming. They got supercomputers that must have told them.

We're really in a sad state of affairs.

I grew up in the Depression, and we had more than they do now. At least you could eat.

Michael, Wabash Avenue Bridge

I was released from Chicago Read Mental Health Center June 18 with $3 in my pocket and no place to go.

When I was released, they told me I would get a welfare check.

They promised, and I got an apartment on that basis.

I went to get the check, and they told me I wouldn't get it, nor would I get food stamps. My caseworker was not in, but I talked to his supervisor. He said the law had been changed and, as a result, I had been cut off.

My landlord, when he found out, took a key and put it in my lock and busted it off so I couldn't get in. All my stuff's there. I have a pair of shorts and a pair of pants and that's it.

There are three dumpsters near here for recycling. One of them is for newspapers. That is where I have been sleeping at night.

I'm 47 and I'm from the Bronx. This is not the first time I have been let out of a hospital with no place to go. The first was from Bellevue when I was 16.

I've worked as a groom at tracks all across the country, and I've worked on horse farms.

I've walked away on a lot of jobs. I never know why. I just have to get up and leave. Lots of times I leave wages there. I've done it all over the country. I don't understand why, but I do it, just get out on the road and move on. I don't know where I'm going or why.

Nelson, Washington Street Bridge

I don't push myself on people. I try to make eye contact and then say, "Have a nice day, sir or ma'am."

Most people just keep walking by, but many are kind. One woman said she'd bring me some information on work I could do on the side. I wouldn't mind that.

I'd rather not ask my family for help, but prefer to go out and do things on my own. I'm 32 and single.

I was in the Marines, a radio operator.

I've been doing this about a year and I told one of my friends about it. He's over on the next bridge.

Clifford Johnson, Monroe Street Bridge

One of the baddest treatments here is that if things are jumping, another panhandler might come over and try to fight for your spot. You can only say, "Move on."

I had a job working nights at a restaurant. I lost it because I was late a couple of times. My landlord was harassing me and wouldn't let me sleep during the day. Then, my landlord illegally evicted me and kept my security deposit.

Now, I stay at a shelter at night.

I don't plan on staying in a shelter forever. I plan on working my way up out of this. I'm going to get a job as a fry cook or a porter.

DeVale Frederick, St. Peter's Catholic Church in the Loop

Mainly, people ignore you. Once a guy gave me a $10 bill, and another time, a guy gave me $20.

What I have to get is $12 a day for a hotel room and something for something to eat.

I've picked up a lot of good friends, people who'll stop and say, "Hello," and put a quarter in. I tell them, "Take care of yourself."

I was hurt 13 years ago. I went to Cook County, and they put pins in my leg. Then, later, it got infected, swelled up and gangrene set in and they had to take my leg off. I was working until they took it off.

I had a family, three kids and an ex-wife. I used to work as a crane operator at Inland Steel.

I hope to get me an artificial leg and a Medicaid card.

Also, what I need is affordable housing.

I eat at Wendy's or Burger King. I am a Catholic.

I go to mass every day here at St. Peter's.

$$15$$

Hurtful Medicaid Cuts in Florida

[A] new study by Harvard researchers ... found that when states
expanded their Medicaid programs and gave more poor people health
insurance, fewer people died. ...
While researchers adjusted the data for economic factors like income
and unemployment and population characteristics like age, sex and
race, and then compared these numbers with neighboring states, they
estimated that the Medicaid expansions were associated with a decline
of 6.3 percent in deaths, or about 2,840 per year for every 500,000
adults added.
—*NEW YORK TIMES,* JULY 26, 2012

In November 2005, Florida CHAIN, a nonprofit consumer health care advocacy organization, asked me to do individual interviews with 16 Medicaid recipients. The Florida legislature, at that time, was seeking to expand the privatization of the federal-state program by forcing recipients to go through profit-driven managed care organizations to receive services. They euphemistically called the experiment, "Medicaid Reform."

The organization, as well as the recipients, perceived that such privatization—like earlier Medicaid cost-cutting plans—would end up being a life-or-death proposition for many recipients. The personal experiences they related in the interviews bore this out.

Despite the efforts by Florida CHAIN, the legislature and governor approved "Medicaid Reform." The federal government—a partner in the program—is, however, now requiring that the state meet certain conditions (as spelled out by Florida's advocates) before approving the expansion.

Three women, who were health advocates in the state, founded Florida CHAIN in 1999. Its acronym stands for Community Health Action Information Network. The organization's purpose is to build common purpose and action among diverse groups on issues of health care access. Its priorities include promoting access to health care for those who are uninsured, underinsured, or supported by government-sponsored programs.

The organization's website is: http://www.floridachain.org/.

Many states today have consumer health care advocacy organizations such as this. The vision toward which they work is that

- people will have unrestricted access to health care,
- people will actively shape their world through civic participation,
- health programs will be designed around people with their participation.

Here are several representative excerpts from those 2005 interviews I did for Florida CHAIN:

Rebecca

I am on Medicaid and Medicare with my bipolar disorder. I also have physical ailments such as type 2 diabetes, high blood pressure, and a brain tumor that put me in the hospital for three weeks and for which I just started radiation treatments. I would definitely be affected if the (Medicaid reduction) bill is passed.

Ron

When I get upset, I write letters. I have written to every president since Ronald Reagan.

I go to meetings with People First. It is a group for those of us with disabilities. They motivate you to think positively and go out and do things

In my group at the center, there were 36 of us, but still we became close. Today, only six of them are still alive. The rest passed away.

I am 40 years old and bipolar, in other words, manic-depressive.

Over the years, I had a couple of jobs doing janitorial work for Burger King and McDonald's. I had to quit when they wouldn't let people work and collect medical disability benefits at the same time.

Three months ago, my friend Marvin Shapiro passed away. We both had talked just before he died about how depressed he was because he was having so much trouble getting his medicine from Medicaid. He said he was going through hell. Then he overdosed and the autopsy found street drugs in his body.

If I could talk to the Governor, there are five things I would ask of him:

- Come and visit the homeless of Broward County, especially in downtown Fort Lauderdale.
- Visit the poor sections of Broward County and explain to the people why he cut their benefits.

- Come walk through the mental health hospitals and see the people who are sick there.
- Talk to persons who have mental health problems and learn from them that they want to live a normal life and not worry about their checks being cut.
- Let me marry my girlfriend and still keep my benefits.
  All we want is to live normal lives.

Manny

My neuropathy starts with real sharp pain and tingling in my toes and shoots up my legs to my hips. The pain is so bad I want to cry. It happens about three times a week. I get massages for it and they help. The government was paying for them three times a week, but they have cut back to twice, and I understand now it will be once a week.

I am on Medicare and receive Medicaid Pac Disability, which pays for medicines.

I don't work. I wish I could go back to work. I volunteer at a nonprofit organization that helps people HIV and AIDS. I was doing it 40 hours a week, but I have had to cut back.

I am part Cherokee and part Puerto Rican.

It was 13 years ago when I was first diagnosed as HIV positive. My first signs had been that I felt weak and nauseous. Then my neck and the left side of my face turned as black as the tar on the road. The roof of my mouth was covered with cancer, Kaposi's Sarcoma. The doctor said if I hadn't been immediately treated for it, I would have died within a day.

Tiffany

I was born with cystic fibrosis, a genetic lung disease. It is not something you catch.

When I was an infant, my parents were told my life expectancy was five years. When I reached that figure, it became 10. The figure for someone born with it today is 32, I am now 33 and my life has not ended yet.

I have two hours every day of pounding on my chest to loosen and bring up mucous from my lungs. I have to strap on a therapy vest four times a day, one that uses air pressure to do the pounding. Each workout is 30 minutes long.

In addition, I inhale three medicines through a nebulizer. This procedure also has to be done four times every day. I take albuterol each time, pulmozyne once, and an antibiotic, colistin, twice. The first session with the nebulizer lasts 45 minutes; the second two, 15 minutes each; and the fourth, a half an hour.

This is my day.

Also, I take 18 different prescription pills. I have to swallow six pills every time I eat because I cannot digest food. Among the others I take are antibiotics and heartburn medicine.

In 2000, right after Christmas, I had a stroke and the doctors discovered a hole in my heart and had to fix it.

Still, I take my kids to schools and do everything I can.

Two years ago, it looked like it was really going to happen. My husband and I went through divorce proceedings so I could retain my eligibility. We told the judge and the people at Medicaid what we were doing and why we were doing it. The judge understood and granted us the divorce "regretfully."

Monty

I am 51 years old, and for many years I was an elementary school teacher.

In 1999, I was diagnosed with MS (multiple sclerosis). My life changed from then on. It is an illness that has many hidden symptoms. The most disabling of them is fatigue, total exhaustion. It can last a whole day, a whole week, or a whole month.

I needed my job, so I kept going after the MS hit me. My only mission every day was to get to work. I would get up in the morning, eat breakfast, go back to bed to get enough energy to wash up and get dressed, do that and go back to bed to get strength to go out to my car, and be exhausted by the time I reached my desk.

There are other hidden problems. Especially at the beginning, I had blurred vision and could not drive. My hearing was bad, and I had a lot of pain, and my right side was partially paralyzed. The drugs I take have helped immeasurably with these symptoms

Four times I applied for Medicaid and disability status with the Florida Office of Disability Determination, but was denied three times before I was finally listed as eligible.

Since then, I have been knocked off several times when the Florida legislature cut back on Medicaid benefits, targeting the particular program under which I was getting help.

Early on, I sold my suits, dresses, and other work clothes. My family gave me groceries, and I got bags of them from the Halifax Urban Ministries, a Methodist organization.

You stay home otherwise. You have no money to do anything. I begged and borrowed, but I did not steal.

Stress also causes problems for people with MS, and if you do not have an income or health insurance and Medicaid does not find you eligible, you have a lot of stress. That time is foggy to me today.

I take an injectable prescription drug, Copaxone. It cost $1,200 a month. Every year, the state legislature reevaluates the list of drugs covered by Medicaid. They took mine off. My doctor was able to get it restored under what is called "prior authorization approval," but time lapses before you get something like that straightened out.

I held up my end of the bargain. I worked, paid taxes, and mistakenly believed I would be protected by a safety net should the need arise. But every year, the Florida state legislature believes that the net should be opened up.

The caseworkers have lost compassion and are forced to look for scams more than to a person's needs.

16

Unemployed

Have you ever told a coalminer in West Virginia or Kentucky that what he lacks is the individual initiative to go out and get a job where there isn't any?
—SEN. ROBERT F. KENNEDY, AUGUST 1964

Republicans, aided and abetted by many conservative policy intellectuals, are fixated on a view about what's blocking job creation that fits their prejudices and serves the interests of their wealthy backers, but bears no relationship to reality.
—PAUL KRUGMAN, *NEW YORK TIMES*, SEPTEMBER 30, 2011

Out-of-Work Steelworkers

In the winter of 1982, the steel industry was hit hard by competition from Japan and the overstocking of steel by the industry. The following laid-off steelworkers had shown up at the union hall to get a free sandwich and a 5-pound box of cheese. Their comments appeared in a Neighborhood Dialogue column I wrote for the *Chicago Tribune* on February 26, 1982.

I wanted to focus on the fact that unemployment is personal. They focused on that, but also emphasized very strongly the economic, social, and—emphatically—the political factors involved in joblessness.

Alice Peurala (president of the local): It is a myth that workers are lazy and want to be on unemployment. They come in here with tears in their eyes. Steel is involved with the economy. When it gets rolling, so will the South Works and South Chicago.

Curtis White: We would rather have reinstated some of the benefits Reagan cut off than be given this cheese they're passing out. There are

61

some jobs out there, but not if you've worked 10 years as a craneman in a steel mill like I have. They ask you about your experience. There aren't any jobs that need 10 years experience in a steel mill. It's hard to find a job when you have no money to go out and look in.

Willie Culver: It isn't fair. We are the people who built this country, built it with our own two hands. I have put 27 years into the steel mill. Something should be done. We are out on the street. We're not asking for something for nothing. We're not looking for a handout. We just want to work, to support ourselves.

James Randall: It's rough. I, too, have been 27 years in the mills. We want to be taxpayers again. Right now I'm living off my vacation money.

Idella Berry: We're getting by, but it's not really getting by. My bills are on hold. I'm filing Chapter 13 bankruptcy. That doesn't feel good. Am I going to lose my house?

Trudy Farr: It looks like a downward spiral for me from now on. The whole thing is not going to open up again for women. We had our few years. I got to work in the steel mills as a result of a consent decree in 1974 that resulted from a lawsuit charging them with discrimination. It was the first time a lot of women went into the mills since the war. We got the chance to get the jobs that paid $8 and $9. We proved we were topnotch workers. They said it would be tough for us. I was a burner. I cut scrap metal with a torch. I found I had power over steel. Did you see the movie, *Rosie the Riveter*? In it, they interview women who worked as welders in World War II and who had to go back to jobs as waitresses or as domestics after the war. One woman was shown looking at an ornamental gate. She said, "I know I could do that." Now, the same thing is happening to me. I am 44 years old. I put a lot into that mill. You know what makes me mad? U.S. Steel makes me mad.

Essie Morgan: My gripe is equal rights for women, too. You know who they're breaking back in? People on "special assignment." And they're not women and they don't have seniority. I had 8 years in. I was a tract mobile operator.

Eloise Webster: In a week or two, I will have exhausted my unemployment benefits. I haven't found any job. I will have to earn $440 more to become eligible again. That's the problem and I hate to face it.

Anthony Prince: The problem is they have overproduced. We steelworkers have been too productive. In comparison with years ago, there were 100,000 fewer basic steelworkers even before layoffs and yet we have set records for steel production. It's a fabrication and a lie that American workers aren't productive. Over 40 percent of all steel produced goes to the auto industry. A small number of companies trying to corner the market have out produced each other. By competing to produce for a profit, they inevitably produced too much.

Bob Jackson: In the steel industry, we have had mismanagement in no uncertain terms. Years ago, they used to go into the rank and file for foremen and supervisors. They got people who knew their fellow employees and their potential. Now, top management is a clique.

Robert Saute: Times have changed in the mills. When I first went to work there, every bearing was greased once every two weeks. There were six people in the oiler gang. When I was laid off last November, the stuff had gone six months without being greased.

Bob Jackson: They talk about workers in Japan and how they don't have to pay them as much. You bet. Japanese workers don't have to earn enough to pay taxes for a big military budget. We supply Japan's defense needs. Of course, their workers come cheaper.

Al Gallegos: I am a veteran. I have spent the last three years as an apprentice at U.S. Steel. I have one more year to become a journeyman. I used up my V.A. benefits for the training.

Henry Soboski: I have been a bricklayer's apprentice for a period stretching over eight years. I have been laid off a dozen times. How am I going to make a house payment? U.S. Steel, in the meantime, called in outside contractors instead of us to reline the glass furnace. They said they could get it done cheaper.

Anthony Prince: If you understand the problem, you are halfway to the solution. Between Gary and Chicago, there are 21,000 steelworkers out of work. There are 80,000 nationally. There is one force in the United States in the position to put them back: The United States government, and it isn't doing it. They are cutting the budget for highway construction, housing, and dams. Where is the money going? Not to food stamps, welfare, and the elderly. Rather to the so-called defense budget, which is actually a pork barrel for big companies. We have the largest military even in peace or war with 40 cents out of every tax dollar going directly for nuclear missiles and the like instead of letting workers spend it themselves for refrigerators and houses. Our local is on record as opposing excessive military spending. All the unemployed in this room are being denied benefits so Rockwell International can build a B-1 bomber.

Curtis White: They talk about budget deficits. Reagan talks about them. Yet, he keeps on sending aid to El Salvador and to all these other dictator governments oppressing poor people. The man in the White House is a beast who is going to turn El Salvador into another Vietnam. People have to come together against him.

Anthony Prince: The problem is we are out on the street. We have skills. We want to work. This country needs steel. The highway system is in ruins. A government study shows that one half of the accidents, 25,000 deaths, happen every year because the highway system is beyond its service life. One out of every five bridges is condemned. Every day it seems like we hear of a derailment because of the poor state of the rails and railroad beds. All these projects need steel, and could put steel workers to work. The steel industry isn't going to do it. There interest is in buying Marathon Oil or diversifying from money they made from our labor. The taxpayers have been subsidizing this industry for years. They shouldn't allow it.

$$\left(17\right)$$

Young, Jobless, and on the Streets

*Nobody asks their names. If it's an older person who might be a cop,
nobody sells to them. Everybody is out there doing it. You see maybe 50
guys in my community on the corner throwing it.*
—ORLANDO CINTRON

This was a Neighborhood Dialogue with the poor of Chicago from
July 16, 1982

Thousands of unemployed Chicagoans were on the streets trying to
find ways to survive. What was open to them was not always legal, much less approved by society. In this interview, two young men
talk about life on the street corner in the West Town and Humboldt
Park neighborhoods. Three others in touch with what is happening there
joined them in the discussion.

The People

Orlando Cintron was 20.

Pedro Perez was 17.

Roberto Caldero, a friend of Orlando and Pedro, is a project director
for the American Friends Service Committee.

Jack Wuest was the director of the Alternative Schools Network, a
citywide coalition of 40 alternative schools, basically serving inner-city
youth.

Anthony Gibbs was a staff assistant for then U.S. Rep. (and later,
Chicago Mayor) Harold Washington (D-Ill.). He had worked with a congressional committee for a year and a half on the relationship of youth
employment programs and crime.

Orlando: I've been unemployed for a year and a half. I worked at
Playskool. I was laid off. I get money. I got my ways.

Pedro: I've been out of work about a year. I've done some work for my cousin off and on by rehabilitating old buildings. But there ain't much of that work.

Orlando: Other guys I know are pushing drugs. They stand on the corners in West Town and Humboldt Park and throw it [deal drugs]. If a person's got good stuff, the customers'll come from everywhere. That's why people try to get the best.

Pedro: Or, you can make it stealing. Stripping cars or just taking what's around, jewelry, that kind of thing. Somebody had a bumper taken off or a fender dented. They ask people to get them a new one and they do. Also, dealers have money and they make good fences for stolen goods.

Orlando: The ones that are stealing aren't doing it from people in the community. They do it from strangers and from people in other communities. But in dealing you got the advantage that you can get your own stuff to be high.

Pedro: On summer days, you can get pretty good business. Some guys make $500 or $600 a week. It depends on the drugs. And it depends on the area. A lot of it's marijuana. But, it's also cocaine ... and pills. The customers drive up in cars. They ride bikes. They walk up.

Orlando: Nobody asks their names. If it's an older person who might be a cop, nobody sells to them. Everybody is out there doing it. You see maybe 50 guys in my community on the corner throwing it.

Pedro: Where I grew up is around Sacramento and Grand. There were a lot of factories around there. If you quit one, you could have always gone to another and get a job. But nobody leaves a job anymore, no matter how bad it is.

Orlando: All my friends are stealing or dealing. They look for jobs, but they can't find them. It's better to work, because of the chance you're going to get caught if you deal or steal, but the only jobs you can get are the slave jobs. That's what they call them in the neighborhood. A slave job is one which you do real heavy labor for the minimum wage. The people say, "The guy's a fool, he could be dealing." I was going to get a job. I was in a CDETA [Continuing Developmental Education and Training Assistance] program for a week. I was getting training to fix up old neighborhood buildings. All of a sudden, Reagan cut it off.

Pedro: Also, guns are a very heavy industry. If you have a good connection for guns, you can really make money.

Roberto: The weapons come mainly from burglaries. The average person has a weapon in his house for protection. It's stolen, and he goes out and gets a new one.

Orlando: When gangs are building up, it's the number of weapons that count.

Roberto: It's just like the arms race between countries.

Pedro: I am out trying to find a job. I have a diploma. Orlando doesn't. It makes no difference. They want experience and they want training.

Orlando: Dealing drugs is like a job. The guys are not all hoggish. They take turns throwing. They watch each other's back when the other guy is throwing. Mostly all my friends are in jail for dealing.

Pedro: There are people who don't ever get caught. I'd say it's 50-50. I know a guy who has been caught 12 times. He spends three nights of the week in jail and the other four he is out dealing. Another dude never had to spend a night in jail. He goes through channels and he has connections.

Roberto: What's out there is worse than I've ever seen it. There's more people on the street corners and they are there all day. They are divorced from the rest of the economy and from the rest of society. The biggest factor is unemployment. It's strange to see that world out there with guys getting up at 10 a.m. and drinking beer and staying out there all day and dealing or stealing or doing nothing.

Pedro: We got to get something. That's why people turn to stealing and drugs.

Roberto: In the community—for us, that's the Near Northwest Side neighborhoods of Humboldt Park and West Town—there have been 476 people killed since January, according to police. People who are dealing drugs are looked up to. They are surviving. They are taking care of their families and their friends. I ask what's going to happen to these people 20 years from now?

Jack: There are 900,000 adults in Chicago without a high school diploma. The unofficial high school dropout rate in Chicago, according to the *Chicago Reporter*, is between 40 and 50 percent. New York's is 45 [percent]. This city in the last seven years has suffered a net loss of 150,000 jobs. The unemployment rate among minority youth is 58 percent in Chicago. Where is it really going to lead to?

Roberto: The worst part is you see guys really go out there and try. You see guys at 7 and 7:30 a.m. hop on a bus maybe four days a week to go to the suburbs to try to find a job. On the average, I'd say it takes a year or a year and half doing that to find a job. That long is not considered unusual at all.

Orlando: People sleep in Humboldt Park just to be first in line to get day labor work from an office there. It's worse than slave labor. The guy who owns the place gets $45 a day each for them. He pays them $25 a day and charges them $2 for bus fare. How can you support a family on $25 a day? That's for the dogs.

Pedro: I've worked daily pay. They sent me to a pizza factory. You carry 80 pounds of pizza around and it's very hot. You burn yourself all the time. I've heard people complain, "I'll never do that again." But the very next day, they are back.

Roberto: You see a lot of people sell things on corners, jewelry and that kind of stuff. And you see them picking up cans.

Pedro: I see 80-year-old men picking up cans. They get 27 cents a pound for them. And I've seen kids mug old men for their cans.

Roberto: People do make money selling drugs. But only a few of them I know have gotten a house and a car out of it. It's small time. Say, the ordinary street corner dealer really keeps at it and does not get busted; he makes maybe $12,000 a year. He has to live with the fear of being arrested and of his supply drying up. Only a few guys make real bucks.

Anthony: Drugs and stealing are job training for organized crime. And believe me, the Mafia is an equal-opportunity employer because that's where the money is. Meanwhile in January 1981, Stanford University did a study of vocational training in big-city school systems. Chicago came out the worst. And they're not doing anything to revamp it. They still have the same people in there. Washburne Trade School is basically for kids from the suburbs. And going there is how you get into unions as apprentices. And take CETA. In the wards and the precincts, they used it as a patronage system. Things have got to change. We got to start looking at things in terms of human values.

Jack: We've got to start talking about where things are headed. We can rebuild neighborhoods dirt-cheap today.

Roberto: There are two different worlds. In one, computers and robots and those who can use them are taking over. You've got to relate that to what's going on the corner. The people there are being edged out.

Jack: What are we going to do with them in the long run? Put them in prisons, on welfare or in mental institutions?

Anthony: Our school system is failing completely. It offers computer training that is 20 years out of date. They're building obsolescence into their classes. The schools are picking up units that IBM no longer wants. We need legislation that will take a new approach.

Jack: Right now, as we switch from a decaying industrial economy to a service-based one, people are being kept desperate enough to take any kind of job. Businesses pay whatever they can get away with and it has a bump-up effect, with plenty of people always willing to take the jobs of the people in the group above them. In the 1960s, society had to provide people with enough money to keep them desperate but cool just enough so that they would not flame up. What do we have now?

18

Our Fellow Americans in Prison

The single greatest cause of prison population growth has been the war on drugs, with the number of people incarcerated for non-violent drug offenses increasing more than twelve-fold since 1980.

At the end of 1980, just before I left office, 500,000 people were incarcerated in America; at the end of 2009 the number was nearly 2.3 million. There are 743 people in prison for every 100,000 Americans, a higher portion than in any other country and seven times as great as in Europe. Some 7.2 million people are either in prison or on probation or parole—more than 3 percent of all American adults!

Penalties against possession of a drug should not be more damaging to an individual than the use of the drug itself.

—FORMER PRESIDENT JIMMY CARTER,
THE NEW YORK TIMES: JUNE 17, 2011

A View from the Inside

My weekly column in the *Chicago Tribune*, Neighborhood Dialogue, allowed various people to speak for themselves about their worlds as they saw them. The following excerpts are from a 1982 group interview of re-imprisoned parole violators in the Cook County Jail.

Grover: Most people think people who come into jail really got to be bad guys. Mostly, they are just trying to survive. A lot of guys with intelligence are in jail.

Earl: Prison makes you slicker. I don't know how to say it except in street language. It puts you onto things. Makes you worse when you are back out on the street. I was in Pontiac Correction Facility. It's all about survival down there. You got problems and you got to deal with them. The penitentiaries rehabilitate nobody. They are only making guys slicker.

Carl: It takes a while sometimes but that is what they do.

Earl: If you are not hooked into a gang, what can you do? You're on your own. I learned a new trade. I learned it in two days. The toilets were leaking. I was given a screwdriver. I was told that if I didn't repair them in two days I'd be thrown in the hole. I learned it.

Johnny: The system is not geared for poor people.

Earl: Take me. I was in the penitentiary. I did a five-year stretch. I went down there when I was 17. I came out with a positive attitude. I wanted to make something of myself. I asked if I could join the service. You know what they told me? We don't accept ex-cons. I laid around. I worked a week or so at a time. I couldn't find anything permanent. I had no skills. I had no alterative but to go back into sticking up and burglarizing. I'm still not giving up. I'm going to school in here right now. I'm still going to try to make something of myself.

Carl: It's getting harder out there. It's getting extra hard. It's getting harder every year. When I got out of the joint, I had a job, but I needed more money. I went back to stealing. What I need is a decent job and I'll not go back to stealing. I'm just like everybody else. As long as a job holds up, I'll stay cool. If it doesn't, I'll stick up or steal. Way things are out there now, things are happening.

Earl: Let me give you an example. You just came out of the penitentiary and you got positive ideas. I went to my parole officer. She says, "Who are you? I don't have any records."

Grover: Right there, that represents a violation of your parole; she doesn't have your records.

Earl: I got that straightened out, and I asked her to help me find a place. She said, "No, my job is just to see you report."

Section 3

WHO ARE THE POOR? THE EXPERTS HAVE THEIR SAY

19

Back When Both Parties Still Seemed to Care

Tens of millions of human beings (those with little opportunity and no money) became invisible. They dropped out of sight and out of mind; they were without their own political voice.
—MICHAEL HARRINGTON, *THE OTHER AMERICA*

In a September 21, 2011 article in *The New Republic*, Isaac Chotiner asked, "Republicans Used to at Least Talk About Poverty. What Changed?"

He cited a time when "the GOP enjoyed displaying a little human tenderness." He spoke of President George W. Bush urging House Republicans not to balance the budget "on the backs of the poor." The article even quoted Newt Gingrich as saying in the early 1990s, "We are going to redefine compassion and take it back."

Those who listened in on the 2011–12 Republican Presidential debates certainly got their fill of the audiences applauding and vocally putting down poor, unemployed, and even the critically ill.

Republicans have stopped short of saying, "I don't care about the poor," but large numbers of them seemingly do not.

What has changed, I believe, is that three distortions in the thinking of many radical conservatives that have caused them to skewer those who are poor. The first is a loss of a sense of oneness as a people and a nation. The second has been the bias of seeing many, if not most of those in need, as less than human. The third is in not seeing them at all, a deceptive position they use to relieve themselves of any responsibility toward them.

An angry hostility against the poor seeks to depersonalize them by projecting them as animals or something less than human. A case in point was an utterance Nebraska State Attorney General John Bruning made in a 2011 campaign speech.

On August 11, 2011, according to The Associated Press, he said while campaigning: "Raccoons are not stupid. They are going to do it the easy way, if we make it easy for them, just like welfare recipients all across the country. If we don't incent them to work, they're going to take the easy way." By way of an attempt at an apology, he later described what he had said as "an inartful statement."

Only invisibility and depersonalization can lead to such horrendous generalizations about those struggling to survive with the help of government assistance. The problem is not so much one isolated commentary but a steady stream of disdain that pours from many on the radical right as well as some media pundits, politicians, corporate leaders, and even—at times—clergy.

Cumulatively, their disdain causes pain, and no one knows this better than the poor themselves.

One mother receiving public aid complained in *They Speak for Themselves*:

> They never hear about the mother who is trying so hard she is neurotic and depressed and don't know what she's gonna do.
>
> Sometimes we just say, "Forget about it." And you go somewhere with the kids. The next day you come home and look at each other. We still can eat, but we cut down on food to make up.
>
> Some people are lazy, but most are trying so hard they don't know what to do. It's like something was breathing down your neck and you don't know what.

How can concerned politicians hope to negotiate on behalf of those in need when they are stuck body and soul in such disdainful attitudes?

And how can they do so if so many Americans today do not see the poor as existing except as strangers in some faraway dangerous neighborhoods?

Those whose efforts are focused on diminishing the poor have borrowed a trick from magician Harry Houdini. They work to make tens of millions of them seem to disappear, and it takes effort for the rest of the country not to be complicit in their attempts.

In 1918, Houdini outdid himself, stunning a New York audience by making Jenny, a ten-ton elephant disappear! We have a record of the event: "The elephant lumbered on to the stage and walked into a large cabinet. Almost simultaneously the cabinet's walls would be pulled back and the elephant had disappeared."

Houdini afterwards told reporters: "Even the elephant does not know how it is done." As Houdini loved to say, "It was hocus-pocus."

In real life, we are the audience. Those who believe themselves above the rest of us attempt—sometimes successfully—to create a major illusion bigger than the hocus-pocus that made Houdini's elephant evaporate. It would seem the 15.9 percent of our fellow Americans who decidedly are poor is too huge a portion of the population to hide. And yet, through some machination, they have seemingly evaporated.

It is not as though they are not visible on occasion. Still, where by the tens of millions are they? Many of us can follow our daily routines on any day and not believe we have seen even one of them while having seen large numbers of them.

They are part of who we are in our nation—they are "we."

In November 2011, the United States Census Bureau announced that the number of people in the 2010 census who had incomes below their poverty thresholds had increased to 49,100,000.

The figure, which took in for the first time rising medical costs and other expenses, increased from the earlier (September) census figure of 46,200,000.

It means that one of almost every six Americans is trapped in a miserable, inhuman situation that causes them deprivation and relentless want. Many analysts believe the figure of those in true poverty is higher.

Sociologists and writers about poverty scratch hard for words to describe the deepest examples of want.

William Julius Wilson, a sociologist now at Harvard, used the phrase, "The Truly Disadvantaged," in his study of harsh poverty.

Brookings Institute defines those who live in very poor neighborhoods as suffering from "extreme poverty."

And Peter Edelman, the director of the Center on Poverty, Inequality and Public Policy at Georgetown University went to the well of words in talking about "the toughest, most malignant poverty that we have in the United States."

The poverty threshold for a family of four is $22,350. This measure recognizes poverty as a lack of key goods and services such as decent housing, groceries, education, employment opportunities, health care, basic utilities, transportation, and clothing along with similar necessities.

Those even poorer, who are living below 50 percent of the poverty threshold, increased between 2009 and 2010 from 6.3 percent to 6.8 percent. These number 20,000,000 or one out of every 14 residents.

Want is not a stagnant situation. Millions sink below or rise above the poverty-threshold every year or few years. This represents, for the most part, people losing or finding jobs, receiving or being cut off government benefits, running into serious medical needs or other life changes. Are these statistics real or an illusion? Are not a lot of these people getting by fairly well? No, they are not.

On March 28, 2011, the *Los Angeles Times* gave a vivid example in the person of Donny Ashley of Watts. He is the father of a family who was poor and then slipped even farther, falling below the poverty threshold, when he and then his wife lost their jobs.

He talked to the paper's reporter about it: "Now I'm drowning. It's a constant feeling of struggle, like no end in sight." The article continued:

> Donny Ashley misses the days when he was just barely poor. Sure, he commuted more than three hours each day to work as an electrical apprentice, but the paycheck—about $575 a week—put his family of four over the federal poverty threshold. But then the economy turned, and he lost his job. His wife managed to get work as a nurse but lost that job about a month ago. Now, having burned through their savings, the Watts family has gone from barely poor to officially poor.

Sometimes, we do see the poor. I was recently standing in a checkout line at a supermarket. The person behind me was describing the situation of a long list of her friends who had lost their jobs, their homes, or both. She had just finished as I completed checking out.

If we are concerned, if we care, if we are personally involved, we might find ourselves

- helping out families in need,
- contributing to the local food banks,
- volunteering at homeless shelters,
- serving food at a soup kitchen,
- visiting the sick and elderly,
- working with church programs providing shelter,
- driving for Meals on Wheels, or
- joining in with those organizations across the country that are fighting poverty.

Some of us campaign for a candidate who we believe will make a difference in the lives of the poor and others who are left behind. More than ever, we fight at the local, state, or federal level against essential safety net programs being eliminated. Others among us get our families or friends involved or we take out a membership in a church group or an organization that is making a difference.

Individuals come together as protestors did in Madison, Wisconsin in the cold winter of 2011 or quietly boycott companies that use near-slave labor and stores that pay unfair wages.

Those of us who are concerned read about the poor and share with others what we have learned. We support National Public Radio, Truthout, AlterNet Hot News and Views, American Progressive Talk Radio, and Reader Supported News, or we join MoveOn.Org. Some help, some organize, some fight, and many do all three.

The Half in Ten campaign offers a plan: *Restoring Shared Prosperity: Strategies to Cut Poverty and Expand Economic Growth.* Information about the campaign is available online at *halfinten.org* and in a later chapter.

People are concerned and do care. And that caring changes the world. It alters the world of the poor and destitute, those just trying to survive. Each and every one who does something positive, no matter how small, work to bring America's unseen elephant up on the stage for the rest of the audience.

One organization—the Coalition on Human Needs (CHN)—is an umbrella group that exists to respond immediately and effectively to the quiet but effective conspiracy that wants to make the poor invisible. Founded in response to Reagan's 1981 cuts in essential assistance programs for those being left behind, it is an alliance of national organizations working together to promote public policies that address the needs of low-income and other vulnerable people.

The coalition's members include people who care about civil rights, about religious issues, labor unions, as well as organizations of those concerned with the well-being of children, women, older people, and those with disabilities. The staff of the coalition is incredibly resourceful and professional in bringing individuals and organizations together. The staff manages to strengthen these people in their efforts to support, defend, individualize, and personalize people in need.

The United States Census Bureau issues poverty statistics each September. At that time, to help make the statistics useful and meaningful, the coalition invites its member organizations and all interested parties to join interactive Internet conferences (webinars). The coalition, however, does more than that. The coalition holds a webinar several days before the information is released to help everyone understand the real circumstances and situations that created the statistics.

The coalition offers a helpful website of up-to-date information on the battle to assist the vulnerable poor. Its staff prefers to talk people rather than statistics. If you care to join the coalition's efforts, you will receive its newsletter, and you can use its resources by visiting www.chn.org. The address of the Coalition on Human Needs is 1120 Connecticut Avenue NW, Suite 312, Washington, DC 20036. Their phone is (202) 223-2532.

If the millions of poor emerge from the invisibility the rest of us have created, it is because we will—as we have in the past—care and do more for and with them. If so, those who treasure equality as a founding principle of this nation can and will work to bring about substantial changes in our society, changes that would provide greater opportunity for them. Their voices will be more concerned about how easily politicians are negotiating away their rights, their votes, and their role in our economy.

Economists such as Robert Reich are reminding us that those left behind—because of their numbers and needs—represent a significant body of potential producers and consumers. If even a portion of them had higher incomes and was spending their earnings to meet their needs, companies might be making more money—and so could we. That might mean

- our kids would have a better chance of going to college;
- our jobs might be more secure;
- our homes, more valuable;
- our taxes, lower;
- our worries, less;
- our outlook, brighter;
- crime, down;
- our family's health, better taken care of;
- our neighborhoods, safer;
- the newscasts, less depressing;
- the propaganda, less shrill and exaggerated;
- our nation, sending a more positive message throughout the world;
- our children's future, brighter;
- our lives—if we stop to think about it—more meaningful.

Which news commentators are genuinely concerned with these possibilities? Which ones offer hope that focus on the individuality of the poor? The poor are strangers only if we want them to be. They are persons without power, only if we are willing to accept them as that.

We can also work to change the economy in innovative ways. In a June 6, 2005 speech, "The Mugging of the American Dream," Bill Moyers challenged

> Believe it or not, the United States now ranks the highest among the highly developed countries in each of the seven measures of inequality tracked by the index. While we enjoy the second highest GDP (per capita in the world excluding tiny Luxembourg), we rank dead last among the 20 most developed countries in fighting poverty and we're off the chart in terms of the number of Americans living on half the median income or less.

In his talk, he became even more specific about what to do:

> Come up with fresh ideas to make capitalism work for all. Ask entrepreneurs to join you—they know how to make things happen. Show us a new vision of globalization with a conscience. Stand up for working people and people in the middle and people who can't stand on their own. Be not cowed, intimidated, or frightened—you may be on the losing side of the moment, as the early progressives were, but you're on the winning side of history. And have some fun when you fight—Americans are more likely to join the party that enjoys a party.

To turn President Reagan's famous criticism of the government upside down toward a more fundamental truth: The poor are not the problem. They are the answer. An awareness of that reality is where our journey starts.

20

The Working Poor

A job alone is not enough. Medical insurance alone is not enough. Good housing alone is not enough. Reliable transportation, careful family budgeting, effective schooling are not enough when each is achieved in isolation from the rest. There is no single variable that can be altered to help working people move away from the edge of poverty. Only where the full array of factors is attacked can America fulfill its promise.
—DAVID K. SHIPLER, *THE WORKING POOR*

Jobs have been the traditional path out of poverty. By itself, employment does not, however, provide a panacea for the multiple problems poverty generates in people's lives or a nation's. First and foremost, a job has to be the means of providing the worker and his family a decent living.

My brother, Father Bert, a Franciscan priest, learned this when he was in charge of the Sacred Heart Parish-run free lunch program in Peoria, Illinois. In recent years, he witnessed growing numbers of the working poor joining the free lunch line that has included upwards of 1,000 people a day.

The program operates between 9 a.m. and 3 p.m. from a downtown rectory window called "Angels' Kitchen." Each visitor receives a sack lunch to take home or eat somewhere else. Individuals, restaurants, and companies donate all the food. A sack lunch includes sandwiches, soup, a salad, and a pastry, if available. Every person also gets a choice of coffee, lemonade, or other beverage offered that day.

"A good portion of the people pick up a bag on their way to work," my brother told me. "It is their lunch for that day. We can tell who they are and that they do it because they need to."

Claire Crone, who works with the program, described those in line as "the hungry who come to us," but then she added that they are also "the homeless, the sick and handicapped, and the underemployed."

People line up no matter how severe the weather, how embarrassed they feel, or how humbled they might be by their public acknowledgement of need.

In seeking the Republican Presidential nomination in 2011, Texas Governor Rick Perry promoted the view that his state could serve as a model in alleviating joblessness. He cited the statistic that, between June 2009 and April 2011, 37 percent of all new American jobs (about 262,000) were created in Texas, and that the state's unemployment rate of 8.2 percent stood below the national average.

An Oct. 20, 2011 *Houston Chronicle* article deflated his proclaimed accomplishment. In addition to paying low wages, it pointed out, the Texas model left people without basic benefits such as health care. It backed this up with figures that showed

> 1.3 million Texas children, or 18 percent, were without health insurance in 2010, the latest year for which statistics are available. The national figure is 10 percent.
>
> Texas leads the nation in the number of uninsured residents overall. Texas also has the third-lowest percentage of people covered by their employers.
>
> An estimated 6.2 million people—26 percent of the state's population, according to the Census Bureau, live without health insurance.
>
> Approximately 49.2 percent of Texans got insurance through their jobs in 2010. That is 6.1 percentage points below the national average of 55.3 and nearly 8 percentage points lower than when Perry took office.

A closer look shows that low-wage positions played the dominant role in this increase in employment.

The Bureau of Labor Statistics has reported that 9.5 percent of these new Texan jobs paid the minimum wage or below, compared with about 6 percent for the rest of the nation. From 2007 to 2010, the number of minimum wage workers in Texas rose from 221,000 to 550,000.

These very low-paid individuals not only still suffer from poverty but also their jobs that pay only minimum wages cause problems—now and in the future—for many of their neighbors and fellow Texans.

In per-pupil spending, Texas schools, for example, rank 44th in the nation.

Poor health care and low-quality schools are not the only problems that large-scale, low-paying jobs perpetuate. Other community issues inevitably arise in housing, infrastructure, over-crowding, a strain on community services, infant mortality, mental health, and crime.

Texas has executed almost as many individuals as the rest of the nation put together. In the process, the state has earned a reputation for having executed people for whom there was substantial evidence that they were innocent.

What has happened in Texas portends a ravaging scourge sweeping across this country.

There and elsewhere, people are going without, cupboards are bare, marital relationships are suffering, any hopes of sending their children to college have withered, and plans for retirement have been squelched.

The excellent October 2011 Half in Ten report, *Restoring Shared Prosperity: Strategies to Cut Poverty and Expand Economic Growth* has outlined the trend the American worker has been facing since the early 1970s.

> For those who do have jobs, there has been a steady decline in job quality over the past four decades. Fewer jobs offer families supporting wages, health and retirement benefits, and the flexibility needed to balance the demands of work and family required to raise children prepared to contribute to our national prosperity when they come of age. Too often, even hardworking individuals with full-time employment face economic hardship because the jobs themselves do not provide the financial means and flexibility required to make ends meet.
>
> Wages are obviously an important component of job quality, but other elements—such as access to training, opportunities for advancement, employment benefits, and workplace flexibility—are all factors of a good job. Comprehensive rethinking of our nation's education and workforce development systems, ensuring these programs place a premium on training future workers, is a critical first step.

Extremely low-paying firms have come to include large corporations, fast-food franchises, landscaping companies, maid services, banks, start-up industries, Wal-Mart-modeled merchandizing corporations as well as manufacturers that once had a reputation for paying decent wages. Many of these are following an economically destructive course of generating huge profits and paying out huge executive bonuses while forcing workers to accept wages nearly equal to unemployment benefits or the minimum wage.

These workers hope, almost certainly in vain, that their severely cut wage situations are only temporary. For many of those looking forward to retirement, this can spell significant limits on their eventual Social Security earnings. They have to use savings they have set aside for themselves, their children's schooling or retirement to support them now rather than later. It is as though a farmer finds himself eating the seeds that were intended for sowing future crops.

To get by, millions of Americans workers today have two and even three low-paying jobs, double up their housing and adopt a measurably different lifestyle than they were accustomed to live. Some find themselves forced to eat at soup kitchens, get canned or boxed foods from food pantries, use food stamp programs and crowd emergency rooms rather than make doctors' visits. One common response to running out of money is not to eat or get past hunger with a short-term diet of popcorn or potatoes.

They also say, "No" to their children and each other in ways they had hoped they would never have to. Understandably, it is not unusual that both the physical and mental health of people decline under the stress of such circumstances.

Some people who are forced to accept wages one-third or one-fourth what they had formerly earned say it can be tantamount to life-long incarceration.

The jobs they find themselves taking formerly had been filled, for the most part, by teenagers or by older people coming back into the workforce. They did not consider that they and large numbers of people supporting families would ever have to apply for low-paying jobs far below their skill levels.

To a large extent, the cause of low wages is a gross lack of concern on the part of some employers for the plight of their workers. Increasingly, firm after firm today vastly overpays executives and underpays their employees.

According to the Institute for Policy Studies, the most recent ratio (2010) for CEOs' pay versus workers' was 325 to 1. The large corporations that these figures represent include banks, financial, oil companies, tech companies, investment and speculative firms, pharmaceutical companies, food processors, major department stores, media companies, fast-food franchises, grocery stores, restaurants, nursing homes, and a great variety of service providers.

Barbara Ehrenreich, the author of *The New York Times* bestseller, *Nickel and Dimed* (Henry Holt and Company, 2008), confronted our nation's lack of concern for the working poor with both her personal experiences and proven facts.

To write her book, she took the cheapest lodgings available and worked as a waitress, hotel maid, house cleaner, nursing-home aide, and Wal-Mart salesperson in cities in Florida, Maine, and Minnesota.

In her evaluation at the end of the book, she wrote:

> ... Shame at our *own* dependency on the underpaid labor of others. When someone works for less pay than she can live on—when, for example, she goes hungry so that you can eat more cheaply and conveniently—then she has made a great sacrifice for you, she has made you a gift of some part of her abilities, her health, and her life. The "working poor," as they are approvingly termed, are in fact the great philanthropists of our society. ... To be a member of the working poor is to be an anonymous donor, a nameless benefactor, to everyone else ...

What is so very readable about her work is that her language and stories cross the gap between the working poor and the rest of society. She wrote about her embarrassment at "peeing in a cup" to take a drug test, and she described the best apartment she could afford.

Many workers are seriously disadvantaged by the weakening of labor unions in collective bargaining for their members, the mass tax benefit-supported outsourcing of jobs, and the threat held over their heads by a company that it might move its operations offshore or from one state to another.

Behind all of this is the powerful political and economic anti-worker philosophy that sustains it. Politicians rely on favor-seeking corporate donations to stay in office. As a result, they have little motivation or willingness to provide the working poor the access or help they give their financial backers. The bleakness of the future comes not so much from the problems of our economy as from the mass political sellout that permits them.

The new conservative movement, in particular, has helped trap the working poor in impossible situations. Its most vocal adherents indignantly fight against the government programs that help prevent needless suffering by individuals with low incomes.

It is difficult for those of us who are not among the lowest income people to understand the differences in their lives and ours. Our lives only occasionally reflect the relentlessness of their:

- endless worry over money,
- unpaid bills,
- empty refrigerators and cupboards,
- transportation that is just not there,
- not making the rent,
- lack of insurance,
- not having even basic dental care,
- having to live out of a car or van rather than in a house or an apartment,
- obsession with ways to increase income or further cut expenses,
- days having to work when sick, and
- illnesses endured for not being able to afford to treat even with over-the-counter drugs.

Sometimes, it is also the little things. One man whom I interviewed in the mid-1960s had a seasonal job putting fruit on fruitcakes for the minimum wage. His comment: "You got to take a lot of little things to keep that job and to keep from going back on relief, but you take them. I like to act human and someone yells at me and I yell back. I can't do that where I work."

Another book that expands on the subject is David K. Shipler's *The Working Poor* (Knopf, 2004). Barbara Ehrenreich called Shipler's book "a powerful expose that builds from page to page, from one grim revelation to another, until you have no choice but to leap out of your armchair and strike a blow for economic justice."

What Shipler does is replace myths and restore personality and character to the millions who work but still live in poverty in America. The book is full of the stories of real people. We see Debra Hall of Cleveland get off welfare and find a job that paid more than welfare did. Fortunately, she was able to live in a two-family house owned by her mother. But she discovers there are added costs, including a car needed to get back and forth to work.

He writes about Wal-Mart, as do many other journalists and chroniclers looking at the faces of poverty in the United States. He calls one of his subjects, Caroline Payne of New Hampshire, "the face of the working poor." She started at the superstore by earning $6.25, "going to $6.80 and sometimes up to $7.50 if she worked at night."

Caroline suffers from something many of the very poor do. She has lost her teeth. Shipler commented, "If she had not been poor, she would not have lost her teeth, and if she had not lost her teeth, she might not have remained poor." He ended his book by observing: "It is time to be ashamed."

Almost all of us involved with our multitiered society know working poor people. Even the majority of extraordinary wealthy often do. They or their corporations hire them as house servants, landscape workers, or as service, sales, or production employees.

But, do we really know the working poor? Could we write more than a one-paragraph guess at what their lives are like?

On occasion as an investigative newspaper reporter, I had the opportunity to observe some aspects of their lives. In one instance, I took a job in a boiler room making phone calls soliciting donations for a police organization, along with minimally employable persons. Other times, I worked at other bottom-of-the-barrel jobs, including at a commercial laundry, and picking cherries with homeless men off Chicago's skid row.

Before becoming a reporter, I worked as a landscaper, in a stainless steel plant polishing pots and pans, and as a door-to-door magazine salesman.

In every one of those jobs, I came to know some of my fellow workers as people whom I respected and about whom I cared.

Still, between us as workers, there was always a profound gulf: I would soon move on while they would be in their jobs the next day, the next month or probably for the rest of their lives. In one instance, it did work out just that way right before my eyes. A relative with whom I worked in the stainless steel factory and who drove me back and forth to work abruptly stopped being available to pick me up. I learned that the reason was that he was hospitalized and subsequently died from a lung disease, one that he developed while working at that factory. I am still troubled that a factory in which I worked could do that to a man.

The job we both worked at called for us to buff pots and pans against a grinding wheel, using an abrasive chemical compound that polluted the air in the process. We were not provided with masks, and the grist and grime simply slipped into our lungs.

I was once undercover in an isolated cherry picking camp near Traverse City, Michigan, where the crew boss wore a pistol on his hip to terrorize us. It was effective.

I once took a job in a laundry that was insufferably hot. The employees had to operate mangles—putting linen through hot, moving rollers—always risking crushing their limbs.

The wages I earned in any of those jobs would not have paid the rent for an efficiency apartment or even for a single room. Nor would the wages have provided me with decent meals, and certainly not the ability to purchase the most basic necessities of life for a family.

I was, for short times, one of tens of millions of this nation's working poor. In retrospect, I was on the bus; but not, as many of them were, under its wheels.

21

The "Undeserving" Poor

Of all the preposterous assumptions of humanity over humanity, nothing exceeds most of the criticism made of the habits of the poor by the well-housed, well-warmed and well-fed.
—HERMAN MELVILLE, JUNE 1854, *HARPER'S NEW MONTHLY MAGAZINE*

In his book *The Undeserving Poor* (Pantheon Books, 1989), Michael Katz powerfully argued that poverty is not the product of poor people's indolence or habits, but rather of a political economy that tolerates and promotes an imbalanced distribution of wealth.

He wrote:

> Within cities, poor people have almost always remained strangers. We pass their houses on a train or in a car; read about them as individual cases; study them as abstract statistics; and encounter them asking for help in public places. ... Most of the writing about poor people, even by sympathetic observers, tells us that they are different, truly strangers in our midst: Poor people think, feel, and act in ways unlike middle-class Americans. Their poverty is to some degree a matter of personal responsibility, and its alleviation requires personal transformation, such as the acquisition of skills, commitment to the work ethic, or the practice of chastity. This "supply-side" view of poverty, often despite powerful evidence, has coursed through American thoughts for centuries. Because this way of talking so pervades American history, I have titled this book *The Undeserving Poor*.

> When Americans talk about poverty, some things remain unsaid. Mainstream discourse about poverty, whether liberal or conservative, largely stays silent about politics, power, and equality. But poverty, after all, is about distribution; it results because some people receive a great deal less than others. ...

Katz's use of the term "undeserving poor" is pure irony, because he disagrees with the term itself. But it is also helpful in pointing to the people whom so many mistake to be unworthy of their basic inalienable human rights. We give them what amounts to a rap sheet that's impossible to overcome, especially if they are handicapped by poor education, racial prejudice, or lack of opportunity.

Ironically, for many the term "undeserving" means such individuals are supposedly lacking in gratitude.

Such an attitude has marked class distinctions almost everywhere back, we can be certain, to the Stone Age. For generations, for example, wealthy and politically powerful Southerners used bigotry to keep in "their place" not only blacks but also poor whites. The customs and laws they initiated and enforced against people of color were technically sparing of poor white workers. Yet, wages and conditions were kept shamelessly low or bad for white workers by reminding them that they were treated better or fairer than blacks.

Those in power often encouraged the Klu Klux Klan and grossly discriminatory laws to harass African Americans to prevent them from ever challenging the wages or status of the low-paid whites. Racial hatred in the South over the last two centuries was passed on by the descendants of those who owned slaves, and it was administered by a system meant to benefit wealthy whites.

That same insidious pattern still exists in the North as well in a disdain for the poor, especially if they are African Americans, Hispanics, or the newest immigrants.

Underneath it all is the propaganda aimed at poor whites to "be content. You are not at the bottom of the ladder, and it is we with our money and power that make certain you are not. We are better and deserve more than you as long as you don't have as much money, power, or prestige as we do." Fortunately, those who recognize this as a cancerous growth in our society are working actively to expose it and fashion a final cure.

For example, in their 1986 pastoral letter, *Economic Justice for All* (# 194, 56), the Catholic bishops presented insight into what we can call meanness toward the poor. The bishops pleaded in part:

> We ask everyone to refrain from actions, words, or attitudes that stigmatize the poor, that exaggerate the benefits received by the poor, and that inflate the amount of fraud in welfare payments. These are symptoms of a punitive attitude towards the poor. The belief persists that the poor are poor by choice or through laziness,

that anyone can escape poverty by hard work, and that welfare programs make it easier for people to avoid work. Thus, public attitudes toward programs for the poor tend to differ sharply from attitudes about other benefits and programs. Some of the most generous subsidies for individuals and corporations are taken for granted and are not even called benefits but entitlements. In contrast, programs for the poor are called handouts and receive a great deal of critical attention, even though they account for less than 10 percent of the federal budget. ...

With respect to error and fraud rates in AFDC (Aid to Families with Dependent Children, a federal program that lasted from 1935 through 1996), this booklet notes that erroneous payments in the AFDC program account for less than 10% of the benefits paid. No more than 8.1% of the families on AFDC received overpayments as a result of client error. In less than 4.5% of all AFDC cases nationally are questions of fraud raised. Moreover, in over 40% of these cases, a review of the facts indicated that there was insufficient evidence to support an allegation of fraud.

A look back in history shows us how bad things can become when we summarily disdain the poor and use the poor against the poorer.

In seventeenth- and eighteenth-century England, and well into the first half of the nineteenth century, British authorities were able to play to an almost universal disdain for the poor by setting up workhouses in which poor people—including even children and old women and men— had to work for their keep or, at best, for a meager pittance.

During this time in England, local parishes were responsible for assigning the poor and destitute to workhouses or finding other means to handle them, including sending them out to work for others pleased to have available unpaid labor.

In one of his reports on a local parish's dealing with the poor, Sir Frederic Eden in his 1797 book, *The State of the Poor* (Benjamin Blom, Inc., reprinted 1929), wrote:

> The poor of St. Martin's Leicester are farmed (out) by a man who receives 14 pounds a week. There are 42 persons, principally old women and young children, under his care. The farmer is a stocking manufacturer and employs the poor in spinning worsted, etc. They work in the summer from 6 in the morning until 8 at night, and in the winter from 7 until 9, meal times excepted. The

house is not well situated, nor aired in the best manner, but appears to be kept very clean. The beds are of flocks, and much infested with bugs.

Many of the poor "farmed out" or sent to workhouses, he wrote, were the wives and children of men conscripted into the army and left with no means to support themselves.

History is full of accounts of how the poor were treated throughout past centuries while others lived in grand wealth and opulence. In order to enjoy superabundance yet tolerate brutal poverty among the ordinary people, it was and is necessary to fabricate the illusion that it is poor people's fault that they are impoverished.

More recently, Charles M. Blow reported in his July 16, 2011 column on the Op Ed page of *The New York Times* some of the ways that the poor find to survive. He described them as

> ... honest people who do honest work — crack-the-bones work; lift-it, chop-it, empty-it, glide-it-in-smooth work; feel-the-flames-up-close work; crawl-down-in-there work — things that no one wants to do but that someone must.

And then he ended:

> They, too, sing America. But they're the ones less talked about — either not glamorous enough or rancorous enough. They are the ones without champions, waiting for the Democrats to gather the gumption to defend the working poor with the same ferocity with which the Republicans protect the filthy rich, waiting for a tomorrow that never comes.

22

Those Who Cannot Afford Transportation

Communities are calling for investment in more mass transit; the benefits will be there for everyone, but especially for the poor.

Transportation has distinct, life-affecting meanings for the poor, the middle class, the wealthy, and almost every economic stage in between.

A homeless man who worked off and on for me called to tell me he was in jail. An individual getting off the "L" [train] had handed him his transfer. A police officer saw it happen and arrested the homeless man when he attempted to use it to save walking the several miles he had to travel.

Two weeks ago, a couple in their late '70s left a grocery store parking lot with a shopping cart fairly full of food. They had figured out how to get past the device, which locked the wheels when you took a cart out of the lot. I gave them a ride and we left the cart behind. Both were using it not only to transport their groceries, but also to lean on while walking the four blocks to their apartment.

A young woman who works at McDonald's gets off work late at night and still walks the mile and half home because she cannot afford the bus, much less a car.

Others—and they are many—cannot afford transportation to go to jobs in the suburbs or, in some cases, back from the suburbs to the city.

Yet on the frequent lists of hardships of poverty we usually read hunger, homelessness, lack of health insurance, or dental care but rarely do we find any mention of lack of money for transportation to get back and forth to potential jobs.

The Chicago-based Center for Neighborhood Technology has taken on the cost of transportation, both public and car ownership, seriously and in depth. Scott Bernstein founded the Center for Neighborhood Technology in 1978, and currently serves as its president. He has frequently testified before Congress on the costs of public and private transportation. President Clinton appointed Scott to the President's Council for Sustainable Development, where he co-chaired its task forces on Metropolitan Sustainable Communities and on Cross-Cutting Climate Strategies.

We invited Scott to present his organization's assessment of the issues involving transportation as they affect the poor in the United States today. At one point, years back, Barack Obama served as a member of the board for Center for Neighborhood Technology.

Poverty and Transportation
BY SCOTT BERNSTEIN

Leave no assistance behind—National policy recognizes the importance of paying for food, housing, and medical care. For means-tested families, these are all subsidized with food stamps, Section 8 housing vouchers, and Medicaid. When it comes to transportation, however, federal policy leaves it up to state and local government to decide whether and how to aid the poor who need help.

Federal tax policy does allow employers to treat up to $120 per month for transit as an employee benefit. Using this policy would create a modest incentive to offer transit assistance instead of offering free parking. Ninety percent of this benefit is claimed in just six regions with mass transit (New York, San Francisco, Los Angeles, Washington DC, Philadelphia and Chicago.) In these regions, less than 10 percent of eligible participants receive the benefits. Working with Cook County this year, the staff of the center has been able to get funds allocated so that employers help workers secure this benefit.

Costs change and so should our policies—When the original poverty income thresholds were set in the 1930s, food cost approximately 27 percent of average income, housing 20 percent and transportation just five, respectively.

While food costs have dropped over the past 30 years, both housing and transportation costs have risen faster than income. Housing and transportation now account for well over half of what low and moderate-income households pay for the cost of living. Federal agencies have just begun to test an experimental "supplemental poverty measure" that starts to correct for these economic changes in our culture, but not transportation.

We pay taxes to support the cost of transportation. Our legislative bodies, however, allocate the bulk of what's collected to streets, highways, and bridges.

A city isn't a desert—Since cities minimize social and physical distance between people and their activities, a city where residents can work, shop, visit, pray, and play by walking or taking transit is a convenient and more affordable place to live, regardless of income. But remove easy access to these essentials and any convenience evaporates and—along with it—affordability.

"Food deserts" describe neighborhoods without supermarkets, while "stretch commuters" describes a journey to work of over an hour. As both of these situations become all too common, the phrases to describe them become a part of our language. The problem has worsened as investment has oozed from the city and inner suburbs to the collar counties and exurbs. Households, unfortunately, make up for the lack of travel choice by using cars, the least affordable option available. Surprisingly, many low-moderate income households now spend as much on transportation as on shelter.

Portland, Oregon started a practice of "walkable amenities" in the late 1970s, one that Chicago has started to copy. Recently, the Chicago Department of Planning started exploring how to link development incentives to filling in these "deserts" with walkable amenities.

Exposed—In a cold climate with leaky homes, we insulate to reduce our need for expensive energy. To lower transportation cost exposure, families similarly need choices, which they can't make all by themselves. These include better street signals, conveniently located stores by friendlier zoning and financing, and a reliable, safe mass transportation. Without such publicly made choices, transit service dwindles and family finances suffer.

One example of such a successful choice involved the Garfield Park neighborhood of Chicago: Faced with the loss of express bus service along Washington Boulevard, residents organized successfully for restoration in the face of it, using the demand the popular Garfield Park Conservatory generated. Then, confronted with the loss of the Lake Street Elevated line, community and suburban leaders came together to rebuild what's now the Green Line service.

Chicago as an example of choices lost—The 49th Ward alderman's office in Rogers Park estimates that when Jewel Foods closed the local supermarket, 3,000 fixed-income households started driving to shop for food. One ward, one store closes, and 3,000 households become transportation cost-burdened.

In Garfield Park on the West Side, in less than a decade, the neighborhood's food choices dropped from 12 stores to zero. People "adapted" either by using the CTA to shop in Oak Park, five miles away, or families carpooled after Sunday services to chase affordable food—up to 30 miles away out the expressway.

Chicago transit use peaked at 366 rides per capita per year in 1926, then dropped during the Depression as street railways went bankrupt; it peaked again in 1946 at 319 rides, then plummeted with the steady abandonment of elevated, streetcar, and electric trolley bus service in exchange for massive expressway and bus investment.

But with every improvement in fares, transfers, and level-of-service, Chicago patronage soared, and with every service loss, ridership dropped and the expense burden increased, particularly on working families and the poor (Werner Schroeder, *Metropolitan Transit Research Study*, Chicago Transit Board 1956, and author's analysis of CTA annual reports to present).

In the year 2000, those earning $20,000–$50,000 per year in metro Chicago spent 55 percent of their income on housing plus transportation (National Housing Conference and Center for Neighborhood Technology, *A Heavy Load: The Combined Burden of Housing and Transportation Expenditures on Working Families*, 2006). But the decade's growth in median income was matched by growth in the combined cost of housing and transportation. This growth left just $51 a month for a household to pay for increases in the cost of food and medical care.

Choices regained—Chicago has rebuilt its Green, Brown, and Blue elevated transit lines. It added the O'Hare and Orange Lines in the 1990s. More recent financial support—enabled by a Transit Future campaign that educated general assembly members district-by-district—has helped meet the Regional Transit Authority's financial needs. Ridership doubled from 1994 to today. Households who use these services get around with one less car, reducing cost-of-living by 10–20 percent.

A nonprofit car-sharing service, I-Go, serves 15,000 member households of all income ranges; it reports that, in the recession, 45 percent of members sold a car within a year of joining; after the recession, that number shot up to 70 percent. Members use the CTA to get to work, one trip out of five, and car-sharing to meet the other 80 percent composed of trips for shopping, getting to school, and visiting. These are good starts, but we have a long way to go, and an effective strategy will require public subsidy for those too poor to pay the tab directly and investment to expand transportation choices.

A way out—Last year's increased gas costs drained $4 billion out of the Chicagoland economy: if we don't act to reduce exposure, the situation only gets worse.

In dozens of cities over the past decade, citizens voted to raise taxes to earn federal, state, and private investment in better transportation. In the past 12 years alone, ballot initiatives—that is people voting to tax themselves to get the resources needed for transit investment—raised $150 billion in cities from San Francisco to Portland, from Minneapolis to Charlotte, from Denver to Salt Lake City.

Such votes last took place in Chicago following World War II. They were to pay for jump-starting expressways, and again in 1973 to create the RTA. It is clear that federal assistance is essential but also that the days of large federal assistance are numbered, and even with a hometown president, federal transit funding gravitates to those cities with "skin in the game."

In 2008, Los Angeles Mayor Villaraigosa boldly led a campaign to secure a new sales tax to enable building 30 years of transit expansion in just 10 years, one-upping Denver's comprehensive effort to build what they called a "Chicago-style system" approved by voters in 2004.

The successful campaigns to secure new transit funding in other cities are always led by local government, and polls show that voters are willing to take the chance on paying for new services led by local or county agencies (John Fairbanks, FMM Polling, personal conversation 2011).

What if we shared—Following Washington DC, Chicago supports a massive bike-sharing program, and could do the same for a form of car-sharing in which households let their own cars get used (for pay) by neighbors when not in use. Since 1996, all full-time college students in Chicago get to ride the CTA for less than a dollar a day using its U-Pass, the only city where a multi-college bulk purchase of discounted passes occurs. If this works for students, we can make it work for the poor and working families too. Real communities work for everyone, but that cannot happen if streets are only managed to increase traffic speeds, and if banks discriminate against locally owned stores within walking distance.

Learning to do it together—By mobilizing our capital to support housing and transportation choices that reduce the cost of living, we just might learn to create an economy that works for everyone. Chicago and Illinois have started to put some of the necessary pieces in place, and these need to be coordinated and better supported; the federal government can use the advent of these experiments to justify appropriating funds to take these ideas to scale. For the sake of poor and working families, there's no time to waste.

Summary

- Communities are calling for investment in more mass transit; the benefits will be there for everyone, but especially for the poor. Our elected leaders should support the call for a referendum on taxing ourselves to expand transportation choice, and sell it as making Chicago affordable for everyone.

- We've demonstrated that communities of students and colleges can bulk-purchase transit passes and lower consumer transportation costs—those same benefits can and should be extended to those who can least afford to pay the tab.

- The recent RTA Reform Act required reporting on progress toward the goals of a system that works for everyone—and that reporting has yet to occur, a situation that needs correcting quickly.

- While the Chicago metro area spends close to 50 billion dollars annually on transportation, just 6 percent of this goes to mass transportation. The bulk of it goes to pay for roads and their vehicles. By shifting more of the total to mass transit, people will drive less, own fewer cars, and lower the cost of living.

- Treating every employer's decision to locate outward, away from where the workforce lives, as a form of desirable "economic development," creates hardships for workers and communities in the form of high transportation costs. High gas prices and an awareness of what all of this costs is starting to reverse the trend, but changes need to happen much more quickly.

- The working poor and working families are in a poverty trap—conditions are such that they have no choice but to pay for extensive and expensive use of cars to get around. This needs to be changed. Illinois passed a law recently requiring that job creation tax credits should only go to companies who locate near mass transit service, and this new law needs to be enforced. Another Illinois law requires that state investments should minimize the combined cost of housing and transportation; this law sets the state's communities up nicely for priority attention under emerging federal policy, too.

- Walter Lippman's dictum, "Democracy means paying attention," was never more true. Disclosing the magnitude of the problem will help support the popular movements needed for political leaders to act.

$$\binom{23}{}$$

Poverty Among Hispanics

BY DENNIS SADOWSKI, CATHOLIC NEWS SERVICE

The following article was published by the Catholic News Service in 2011.

Bundled against a gusty, cool autumn wind, Natalie Garcia and her boyfriend, Geraldo de Jesus, make their way across the parking lot outside of the Sister Regis Food Cupboard, a cart full of groceries in tow.

Canned green beans, pasta, spaghetti sauce, bread, cereal, juice, and baby formula for Garcia's 6-week-old son, Joseph, are among the choices from the food center's shelves. Garcia, 24, expects the food to last a week, perhaps a little longer if de Jesus, 30, gets a few days of work as a handyman.

Natives of Puerto Rico, both Garcia and de Jesus are recent arrivals to the Hispanic community encircling St. Francis Xavier Cabrini Parish in Rochester, N.Y. Garcia, 24, arrived from Chicago in November, looking for a new start in a smaller, less congested and less expensive city. De Jesus, 30, came to town with a friend in 2009 seeking work, hoping the economy was a bit better and jobs more plentiful. So far, he has found that jobs for someone who did not finish high school are few. In a typical month, he'll earn about $500.

Garcia and de Jesus represent the growing number of Hispanics living in poverty. U.S. Census Bureau statistics for 2010 show that 26.6 percent of Hispanics—13.2 million people—are poor. The figure represents a 1.3 percent increase from 2009.

Garcia, who also left high school before graduation, has learned to get by on public assistance and food stamps. Life, she admitted, is far different than when she earned $11 an hour as a nurse's assistant in Chicago.

"This is my first time on public assistance," she told Catholic News Service Oct. 3 while waiting for her name to be called by volunteers at the food cupboard. "I have always provided for myself. I've always been very independent."

Garcia said she wants to get a GED and find work in health care again, but those prospects have been put on hold so she can care for her son. For now, Garcia and de Jesus are thankful for the efforts of people such as Mercy Sister Julia Norton, Sister Regis Food Cupboard director, to ease them through this tough time.

For Sister Julia, the couple's story is typical. She has seen a growing number of young Puerto Ricans, Mexicans and blacks troubled by a lack of jobs.

"My numbers have almost tripled," she said of the 850 households who now visit the pantry every month compared with her first days on the job in 2008.

Never a prosperous neighborhood, Northeast Rochester is experiencing some of its greatest economic challenges since Sister Julia arrived 38 years ago to minister in the city's Hispanic community.

Using state and federal data, Action for a Better Community, New York's network of community action agencies, found that the Hispanic poverty rate in Rochester stood at 43.2 percent in 2010, the highest it has ever been.

"There's still an awful lot of single parents, an awful lot," Sister Julia said. "And there's an awful lot of men coming in. The majority is Hispanics as far as I can see. If you look at the schools here in Rochester, the Hispanics, the majority are not even finishing high school."

"That's the main thing that keeping the Hispanics so poor. It's keeping the next generation poor," she said.

Census Bureau data also shows that the number of poor Hispanic children in the U.S. jumped 8.9 percent in 2010 to 6.1 million, surpassing for the first time the number of poor white children at 5 million. In contrast, 4.4 million black children were poor.

An analysis by the Pew Hispanic Center in Washington attributed the rapid rise in poverty among Hispanic children to the growing number of Hispanics overall, high birth rates and declining economic fortunes.

With the poverty comes a wide range of social ills: substance abuse, prostitution, unattended children at home and the rising incidence of diabetes and other serious illnesses that result because people do not have health insurance and do not address symptoms when they first arise.

Priscilla de Jesus, pastoral minister at St. Francis Xavier Cabrini Parish, said many more people have asked the church for assistance in the last three years since the recession hit. She has worked in the Hispanic community for 28 years since leaving Puerto Rico with her husband in 1983.

"(People) are not very comfortable. People call me. They say they need help to pay rent. Some time they say 'I can't find a job. Can you help me?'" she said.

"I would like to do more for them. I try to be with them at the time. I try to counsel them. Everything that I can do for them, I've been here for them. I've been very open for them," added de Jesus, who is not related to Geraldo de Jesus.

Father Laurence Tracy, 71, a retired priest with long-established ties to the parish, continues to minister on the streets of Northeast Rochester. He sees poverty becoming more deeply entrenched, reaching across generations. For today's Puerto Ricans, many of whom are the descendants of those who came north beginning in 1946 in pursuit of jobs in clothing manufacturing and food processing, the prospects of well-paying employment are dim.

"Poverty has gotten systemic," Father Tracy told CNS during a break from his ministry on the streets. "It's no longer a temporary problem. It's endemic to our economy."

So what gives people mired in poverty hope?

Pointing to the papal social encyclicals, Father Tracy said the church has long talked about the importance of people of faith helping each other and working to overcome social injustice.

"That comes naturally to poor people, especially Latino poor people, the cooperative effort to help one another in your family and your community," he said. "There's a lot of sharing that goes on. I think it's in inverse proportion: the worse things get, the stronger this socialization."

Father Tracy knows that's not an adequate solution, but for now, he said, "That's about the best people have."

$$\textbf{24}$$

Race, Place, and Poverty

BY ANGELA GLOVER BLACKWELL, FOUNDER AND CEO, POLICYLINK

PolicyLink is a national research and action institute advancing
economic and social equity; the following article appeared August
31, 2010 in *Spotlight on Poverty: The Source for News, Ideas and
Action,* an initiative managed by CLASP (www.clasp.org).

At no time in recent American history did the intersection of race,
place, poverty, and policy become more shamefully evident than
during the events surrounding Hurricane Katrina. The storm and the
catastrophic flooding exposed black suffering and government neglect
to a shocked public and sent a message to everyone who cares about
building a just, prosperous nation: we must change the counterproductive
and dangerous way we have created and inhabit many of our cities and
regions, excluding people of color from opportunity.

That deep poverty exists, that it is concentrated primarily in black and
brown communities, that disinvestment of low-income neighborhoods of
color perpetuates disadvantage across generations was not news to the
millions of people living in such places. But the searing images of New
Orleans—bodies floating in the floodwaters, families stranded on rooftops, the sea of desperate faces in the Superdome—jolted many Americans from the blind complacency of their suburbs, their gentrified urban
enclaves, and other affluent communities where it was possible to tell
yourself that ours is a land of opportunity for all.

America was forced to recognize that, for Black America, far too little
has changed since the civil rights struggles of the 1960s. Despite antipoverty efforts, our nation had not addressed the fundamental factors that keep
people poor. To lift people out of poverty and make good on the promise
of opportunity for all, we must honestly and authentically confront our nation's deepest fissure and most entrenched barrier to equity: race.

That learning has propelled the nation onto new terrain, where policymakers, funders, advocates, and the public increasingly recognize race as an overarching consideration that affects every aspect of society. This new terrain isn't always comfortable. Discussions of race add a layer of complexity to policy and politics that many people are unaccustomed to, and uneasy about, confronting directly. And sometimes the terrain is downright ugly—just ask Shirley Sherrod.

Yet this new landscape offers tremendous opportunities for building a nation that is more just, fair, and inclusive. It points the way toward strategies that have the potential to transform distressed communities into socially and economically vital places where all residents can participate and prosper. By crafting solutions based on a clear understanding of the connections among race, place, and poverty, we have a chance to get things right.

Five years later, this essential lesson of Katrina is informing action at all levels, from the federal government to the streets of New Orleans. The Obama administration is spearheading bold, comprehensive, place-based initiatives to increase opportunities available in vulnerable communities and achieve broad improvements in the well-being of residents.

For example, the Sustainable Communities initiative will help regional consortia lay out a smarter, more environmentally sound, and more inclusive future for entire regions. The Promise Neighborhoods and Choice Neighborhoods initiatives leverage and combine the resources of programs that have historically operated in distinct spheres—neighborhoods and education in the case of Promise, and housing, transportation, economic development, and education in Choice—to break the cycle of generational poverty.

By targeting high-poverty areas, these programs zero in on communities of color. And by focusing simultaneously on people and the places they live, these programs avoid the past mistakes of antipoverty efforts that invested either in physical makeovers of neighborhoods while leaving residents high and dry, or in services to individuals without addressing the environmental factors crucial for sustained advancement.

These federal initiatives hold real hope for changing the life trajectory of poor children of color for generations to come. They must be fully funded.

A growing number of foundations, too, are directing resources at the nexus of race, place, and poverty. As a starting point, they are grappling with long-unspoken questions about skin color and ethnicity. What roles have bias and racism played in the disinvestment of communities? In the inequitable delivery of services? In the widely disparate outcomes in health and education, two areas of longstanding concern to philanthropy?

The Open Society Institute's Campaign for Black Male Achievement, for example, addresses the exclusion of black men and boys from social, educational, and political life. The Kellogg Foundation recently launched a five-year, $75 million initiative to improve outcomes for vulnerable children and their families by promoting racial healing and eliminating barriers to opportunities—and received nearly 1,000 proposals for funding.

A similar shift is happening at many think tanks, community organizations, and advocacy organizations dedicated to fighting poverty. Race was for so long an untouchable consideration. At last people are engaging the subject forthrightly. Katrina jolted even veterans of antipoverty struggles into recognizing that African American poverty is a special problem, rooted in a history of racism older than the country itself and supported by inequitable structures and systems that undergird communities like the steel skeleton of a skyscraper.

But those structures and systems can change. Just as Katrina opened the nation's eyes to African American suffering, bottom-up recovery efforts are showing us the resilience and enormous potential of low-income communities. The best of the recovery work has capitalized on the rich cultural and aesthetic assets of New Orleans and the Gulf region. Residents, advocates, volunteers, and faith organizations have kept the spotlight on the disparate impact of the disaster on African Americans and the dire needs yet to be addressed.

The work has gone beyond a single fix—for instance, housing restoration, critical as that has been—to press for the services and opportunities that make a place the kind of community we all want to live in—a community with high-quality schools, grocery stores, transportation, health clinics, and parks. Innovative projects are emerging as models of equitable development. In the process, residents have discovered their voice, their imagination, their power.

The rest of the country needs to pay attention to the lessons from the Gulf region today, as we did five years ago.

25

Native Americans Who Are Poor

BY TOM RODGERS

Tom Rodgers is the president of Carlyle Consulting of Alexandria, Virginia. A Blackfoot tribal member, he advocates on behalf of Native American tribal governments and their people. He was previously a congressional staffer for Senator Max Baucus. The following article appeared in Spotlight on Poverty: The Source for News, Ideas and Action, *an initiative managed by CLASP (www.clasp.org).*

To be a poor man is hard, but to be a poor race in a land of dollars is the very bottom of hardships.
—W.E.B. DU BOIS

No discussion of poverty or of the need to renew opportunity in America can be complete without a frank consideration of the situation faced by Native Americans. With a worsening economy, the inevitable churn of holiday stories about the least fortunate, and a new Administration, now is the right time for meaningful action to address poverty in Native American communities

The modern history of Native Americans has been marred by tragedy and injustice, and too often deprivation and suffering within Native American communities has been met with sentiment that shocks the conscience

In 1862, the American government refused to honor treaty obligations to the Dakota Sioux Indians during a time of widespread starvation. When tribal leaders, desperate for relief, asked for food on credit because the U.S. government had failed to provide moneys owed, an associate of the local Indian agent replied, "If they are hungry, let them eat grass or their own dung." His comment, and the crass disregard it represented, helped to spark the infamous and bloody confrontation between the tribe and the federal government now known as the Dakota War.

Although we have moved beyond wanton neglect and violence, our national response to the problem of poverty in Native American communities remains woefully inadequate.

The extent of the problem may not be well known. American Indians and Native Alaskans number 4.5 million. According to the U.S. Census Bureau, these Americans earn a median annual income of $33,627. One in every four (25.3 percent) lives in poverty and nearly a third (29.9 percent) are without health insurance coverage.

To put this in stark terms, counties on Native American reservations are among the poorest in the country and, according to the Economic Research Service at the U.S. Department of Agriculture; nearly 60 percent of all Native Americans who live outside of metropolitan areas inhabit persistently poor counties.

Contrary to popular belief, the overwhelming majority of tribes are not wealthy by virtue of gaming. This is mostly attributable to a fact, which all sovereign nations have come to understand, that geography is all too often destiny.

For most tribes, their remotely placed homes and communities frequently stifle viable economic activity. This disturbing result is particularly harsh when we recognize that Native Americans witnessed their geography chosen for them by those who sought to terminate them as a people.

A major cause of poverty in Native American communities is the persistent lack of opportunity. The Economic Research Service reports that Native American communities have fewer full-time employed individuals than any other high-poverty community. Only 36 percent of males in high-poverty Native American communities have full-time, year-round employment.

On the Blackfoot Reservation in Montana, for example, the annual unemployment rate is 69 percent. The national unemployment rate at the very peak of the Great Depression was around 25 percent. That means that each year the Blackfeet people, whose aboriginal lands once comprised Glacier National Park, suffers an employment crisis nearly three times as severe as the Great Depression.

One does not need to travel to a developing nation to find extreme poverty. It is here, in America. In our own backyard.

Yet beyond these bleak statistics, there is very little discussion of the causes of Native American poverty and what to do about it. The sad truth is only a handful of policymakers give Native Americans priority on the national agenda. Few even know that November was Native American Indian Heritage Month and that, by Congressional resolution, the Friday after Thanksgiving is Native American Indian Heritage Day.

In a time for giving thanks, we too readily forget that one of the first stories behind Thanksgiving dates to 1621, when it is said to have been celebrated by the pilgrims at Plymouth and the Wampanoag tribe of Massachusetts.

In addition to their symbolic exclusion from the table, America's indigenous populations have struggled for recognition. Most of the world's nations have been reluctant to take positive steps to support the rights of indigenous peoples. The United Nations Permanent Forum on Indigenous Peoples set a goal early this century for adoption of the Declaration on the Rights of Indigenous Peoples. In 2007, 143 countries finally adopted the declaration. The United States—the wealthiest country in the world— was not one of them.

Expanding formal rights is important, but we also need better federal performance on these issues. The Government Accountability Office (GAO) has leveled a number of criticisms at the agencies responsible for federal Native American policy, including "long-standing financial and programmatic deficiencies" in the Interior Department's American Indian programs. A 2006 GAO report also found that the Office of the Special Trustee for American Indians has failed to implement several key initiatives specified by the American Indian Trust Fund Management Reform Act of 1994, including establishing an actual timetable for completing its mission.

The government should also take more aggressive action on providing essential services and the necessary tools for effective self-governance to Native American communities. Congress has failed to reauthorize the Indian Health Care Improvement Act since 1992. Initially passed in 1976, the Indian Health Care Improvement Act was designed to bring the waning health of Native American communities up to the standard enjoyed by all Americans.

Section 4

LET'S DO SOMETHING

The poor want a slice of the loaf and the right to earn it. They need adequate, earned wages. They want to fulfill the role of producers and consumers in our economy. They seek opportunity and jobs, ones that carry with them dignity and the means to put food on their tables, a roof over their heads, health care, a decent education for their children, and a comfortable retirement.

"We are not talking simply benevolence or even justice," former Labor Secretary Robert Reich said on this point, "but most emphatically, a much-needed functioning economy."

26

Social Security, Medicare, and Medicaid

Poor men's reasons are not heard.
—THOMAS FULLER

To many conservative Americans, cutting government support in administering the entitlement programs of Social Security, Medicare, and Medicaid or changing to a voucher system is a must do.

To them, basic cuts and risky changes in services to end the programs as our parents and we have known them are the cure-all for lowering the nation debt and rescuing the programs themselves. They are more than willing to let more middle- and low-income people survive on a lot less in the future.

They are willing to postpone some of the most immediate harm by delaying their proposed changes in Social Security so they would affect only those starting to receive benefits in the future. But such is the full extent of their response to the call for mercy.

These conservatives fail to look to the individual well-being, survival needs, and basic economic protection these programs have provided millions of Americans over the last 70 to 80 years. They fail to take into account the faith that generations of people in hard and good times have successfully placed in these three programs over the years.

If you replace the calculator of faith in the future with one that registers only fear, the figures come out very different and will continue to do so no matter how much you cut them back.

Each is a reasonable and necessary dam constructed to hold back the devastating floodwaters of poverty that constantly threaten to overwhelm older and disabled American citizens. Social Security eliminated the tragic poorhouse from our country. Medicare and Medicaid, for example, have been major reasons that the proportion of elderly Americans living in poverty, which had been 35 percent in 1959, dropped to a record low of 16 percent by 1971.

In 1959, I joined other volunteers at the Detroit free medical clinic. We surveyed the residents of high-rise public housing for the elderly about their health needs. The results overwhelmed us. Every single unit we visited reported at least one person having serious, untreated medical problems.

What if congressional Republicans had severely cut these programs several times in the past? They would still be calling to do it more today and again in the future. Their proposed cuts are not a one-time thing. We can be certain they will be repeated in the future.

These programs serve as a dam. Putting a hole in it is a very dangerous thing to do.

Here is a list of some significant reasons for not cutting these programs or changing them into precarious voucher ones.

1. **The California Public Policy Center has called the damage being done to the pension plans that have protected the ordinary American worker more like the tsunami that struck Japan than a mere crisis.** Tens of millions, when they reach retirement age, will have little—if anything—to fall back on. With little room to avoid that disaster, the proposed cuts in these programs, long-term, will mean grinding poverty.

2. **The poor farm alternative.** The only real backup for the United States would be to reinstitute the poor farms with their large, attached cemeteries if older or disabled people

    a. cannot afford to live on their Social Security income,

    b. cannot meet their medical bills, or

    c. lose on their vouchered payouts.

3. **Social Security helps keep 20-plus million Americans out of poverty.** The powerful fact about Social Security, according to a 2007 article by C. Sturr and R. Vasudevan (editors) in Current Economic Issues, is that it keeps roughly 40 percent of all Americans age 65 or older out of poverty. This would entail 21,600,000 of the 54,000,000 Americans who were receiving Social Security presently. The figures do not include those saved from abject poverty by Medicare or Medicaid. How fewer would be rescued from real poverty if Congress goes through with the cuts? We would have a very different country as a result.

4. **Social Security, Medicare, and Medicaid together represent a test of our nation as a people.** Driven more by ideology rather than a concern for real people, the present-day conservatives very often do not appreciate the misfortune of our older fellow citizens. The Paul Ryan Plan sees them as ciphers and ignores them as individuals. Abraham J. Herschel, who saw the Hebrew prophets and religion as a clarion call for social action, warned: "A test of a people is how it behaves toward the old. It is easy to love children. Even tyrants and dictators make a point of being fond of children. But the affection and care for the old, the incurable, the helpless are the true gold mines of a culture."

5. **Lives would be at stake by the tens of thousands.** According to the National Committee to Preserve Social Security and Medicare,

> Social Security is the most common source of income for older Americans. Of the money received by older people, four dollars in ten come from Social Security. Only half of married couples and less than one-third of unmarried women receive income from pensions or annuities. Only one-in-three elderly couples and one-in-six unmarried women receives $2,000 or more a year in income from other assets. These amounts help considerably most of those on the fixed incomes after retirement by supplementing pensions, savings accounts, or IRAs. ... What Congress needs is to perceive those who collect Social Security not as a body of 54,000,000 recipients but as individual persons whom the proposed cuts in benefits would affect in radically different ways. For some, enormous hurt and even their lives could be at stake.

6. **If we keep those Americans citizens receiving Social Security payments above the poverty line, we keep a real, continuing stimulus flowing into our economy.** Older Americans are far more likely to buy American-made products and create jobs rooted in our country. These individuals tend to appreciate American workmanship and the products we produce both locally and nationally. They understand the economy in ways young people often fail to grasp. The National Bureau of Economic Security on its blog states: "While poverty was once far more prevalent among the elderly than among other age groups, today's elderly have a poverty rate similar to that of working-age adults and much lower than that of children."

7. **The three major proposals to save money by burdening Social Security recipients lack any appreciation of why and how it has worked.**

Proposal A. Increasing the retirement age –

It hurts those large numbers of people laid off in their fifties and sixties and not able to find jobs. The idea is just plain cruel to them.

Proposal B. Reducing the cost of living adjustment (COLA) –

This is equally, if not more, cruel to those who receive only enough from the program to eke out a living and avoid personal, physical, and mental consequences. How can they choose to put the responsibility on these individuals to make sacrifices rather than on the wealthy?

Proposal C. Increase the averaged numbers of years that determine one's benefits –

This proposal saves money by doubling down on the problems that caused lay-offs, sickness, childbirth, or other complications that commonly affect workers in their jobs.

An available solution:

Lift the cap upward from its present \$106,800 and include all—all—taxable income. According to Harvey Rosen and Ted Gayer in their 2008 book, *Public Finance*, this simple change will lead to solvency for Social Security. The challenge is to convince the radical Republicans and Libertarians through the voice of the public that helping those in need instead of the rich is not a wrong thing to do, but rather the right one.

27

Are You Scared?

> It's a puzzle: one dispossessed group after another—blacks, women, Hispanics and gays—has been gradually accepted in the United States, granted equal rights and brought into the mainstream.
>
> At the same time, in economic terms, the United States has gone from being a comparatively equalitarian society to one of the most unequal democracies in the world.
>
> —ALEXANDER STILE, *THE NEW YORK TIMES*, OCTOBER 23, 2011

The year 1942 was the scariest year of my life. I was eight years old and the United States was engaged in a really big world war, and we were not winning. And we might not.

In my bones, I knew it. It was like the first or second inning, but the other guys were getting all the hits and our team was making all the errors. We were going to lose the big, big game.

It was only idle to think that it did not matter or that—like a scary ride in an amusement park—it would suddenly end and we could get off. Our brave soldiers on Battaan and Corregidor were being mowed down and taken prisoners like nobody's business. American ships carrying supplies to England were disappearing from the surface, sunk by submarines like the soap bubbles popping in my bathtub.

The good news was that everybody was joining the army and the navy, and lots of guns and ships were being made to replace the ones that we were losing. Still, the hope all this gave me lasted only until the next newscast on radio station WCAR.

We had to win. We had to. It was more important than if you together the worst possible fears about all the Detroit sports teams to which I had pledged my loyalty.

I did not want some other country to take over America, my city of Ferndale, Michigan or my home at 545 Ardmore Drive. I felt the war was a very personal fight. Even though I was only eight years old, I knew that if I did not do everything I could, we might lose it. I joined what was called "the war effort." I saved tinfoil and wrapped it up in a big ball, helped take old newspapers to the paper drive, got a war savings stamp booklet, spent my movie money, 10 cents, for a stamp that I pasted into the book. My actions did not win the war, but it was not for lack of trying on my part.

I deeply believe today that, in forfeiting equality by leaving behind tens of millions of Americans, our nation is losing a war that counts for everything, our struggle in behalf of "liberty and justice for all."

And I feel, no less today, that the fight is personal. This one is for equality and on behalf of those whom we know are left behind. Together we can take it on our shoulders—no matter how broad or narrow they might be—and turn this terrible unfairness around. My nation, my city and my home will be lost as if "liberty and justice for all' in the Pledge of Allegiance are mere words

- if the poor and the destitute and their children continue to become poorer and keep doing so in astronomical numbers;
- if an ordinary citizen no longer can grab even a piece of the American Dream;
- if we no longer keep the elderly out of poverty as we have through Medicare and Social Security;
- if little children, like those in this book's foreword, have to keep burning candles because their family cannot afford electricity;
- if health care continues to be seen as a privilege rather than a right;
- if tens of millions of people are limited in job finding because they cannot afford or find public transportation.

In a Reader Supported News column on their website on September 14, 2011, Senator Bernie Sanders of Vermont, an independent in the U.S. Senate, commented:

> ... [P]overty in America today leads not only to anxiety, unhappiness, discomfort and a lack of material goods. It leads to death. Poverty in America today is a death sentence for tens and tens of thousands of our people, which is why the high childhood poverty rate in our country is such an outrage.
> Some facts:
> - At a time when we are seeing major medical breakthroughs in cancer and other terrible diseases for the people who can afford those treatments, the reality is that life expectancy for low-income women has declined over the past 20 years in 313 counties in our

country. In other words, in some areas of America, women are now dying at a younger age than they used to.

- In America today, people in the highest income group level, the top 20 percent, live, on average, at least 6.5 years longer than those in the lowest income group. Let me repeat that. If you are poor in America you will live 6.5 years less than if you are wealthy or upper-middle class.
- In America today, adult men and women who have graduated from college can expect to live at least 5 years longer than people who have not finished high school.
- In America today tens of thousands of our fellow citizens die unnecessarily because they cannot get the medical care they need. According to Reuters (September 17, 2009), nearly 45,000 people die in the United States each year—one every 12 minutes—in large part because they lack health insurance and cannot get good care. Harvard Medical School researchers found in an analysis released [recently that:]
- In 2009, the infant mortality rate for African-American infants was twice that of white infants.

I recite these facts because I believe that as bad as the current situation is with regard to poverty, it will likely get worse in the immediate future. As a result of the greed, recklessness, and illegal behavior of Wall Street, we are now in the midst of the worst economic downturn since the 1930s. Millions of workers have lost their jobs and have slipped out of the middle class and into poverty. Poverty is increasing.

Further, despite the reality that our deficit problem has been caused by the recession and declining revenue, two unpaid-for wars and tax breaks for the wealthy, there are some in Congress who wish to decimate the existing safety net which provides a modicum of security for the elderly, the sick, the children and lower income people. Despite an increase in poverty, some of these people would like to cut or end Social Security, Medicare, Medicaid, food stamps, home heating assistance, nutrition programs and help for the disabled and the homeless.

The above is printed with the permission of Senator Bernie Sanders

Fortunately for this nation, for the poor, for you and for me, people like Senator Bernie Sanders exist and are fighting to restore the egalitarian heritage of this country and—if the nation can come together to do that—the scary ride will end and we can all get off safely.

28

Jobs in Rebuilding America's Infrastructure

Magnificent things have been accomplished in Laurel [Mississippi] by WPA workmen. The [high school] stadium is one example; others are found in schools repaired, sidewalks built, parks and school grounds improved. But there have been changes not so apparent: changes in the hearts of men who were discouraged and unhappy, and are no longer; in whom hope is revived and life once more holds promise.
—*LAUREL LEADER CALL*, AUGUST 29, 1936

Millions of us want to get the best benefits and the longest-lasting value from our property. We invest whatever resources and labor we have in order to improve it, make it last and to continue to hold its value. Otherwise, tomorrow or next year, its worth may come tumbling down—and its value and even its potential might be gone.

It is a truism that the greatest assets in which we need to invest are our people. The Depression-era Americans understood this and found ways to borrow money from the future to invest in both the nation's infrastructure and its people.

We, who stand in their future by several generations, have every reason to appreciate and be grateful for the lasting results they achieved and the courage they demonstrated in doing it. And, I believe, the time will come in the future when other generations will look back upon this one and question whether we made such decisions with an equal amount of courage or whether our timidity did not allow us to do so.

It will hopefully be out of love and not just fear that we prove willing to pledge our assets and go into temporary debt to protect and provide for the future. The April 9, 2008 issue of *Popular Mechanics* reported:

> Americans need to face the sobering reality that the country's infrastructure is in trouble. Most of it was built in the 20th century, during the greatest age of construction the world has seen. The continent was wired for electricity and phone service, and colossal projects, including the Hoover Dam, the Golden Gate Bridge

115

and the interstate highway system, were completed—along with thousands of smaller bridges, water tunnels and more. We are living off an inheritance of steel-and-concrete wonders, grander than anything built by Rome, constructed by everyday giants bearing trowels, welding torches and rivet guns.

Sound economists are urgently trying to tell us we can resolve two gnawing problems of restoring the infrastructure and creating jobs in the same swipe. We could end the high unemployment if the government hired those in need of work to fix bridges, roads, and public buildings.

As a nation, we desperately need decent jobs now—not just for the benefit of the unemployed and their families but also to keep the economy and our country functioning.

We have an example in the Works Progress Administration (WPA) of the 1930s, which put 10 million Americans back to work during the Depression even while renewing and improving the structures and assets of our nation.

The jobs are needed but the bias is not. Because the very wealthy controlled so much of the media in the 1930s' version of the one percent, papers repeated over and again the anti-Roosevelt and anti-New Deal myths maligning the WPA. And they felt it their mission to preach their own deep-rooted distrust of ordinary, working-class Americans, especially those out of work. The WPA workers had to fight newspapers, magazines, and radio stations that carried propaganda saying you could not trust an ordinary laborer to work without a forceful foreman threatening him with the loss of his job.

In his excellent study of the WPA, *American-Made: The Enduring Legacy of the WPA: When FDR Put the Nation to Work* (Bantam Dell, 2008), Nick Taylor wrote:

> One final accomplishment of the WPA's (Works Progress Administration) must never be forgotten. These ordinary men and women proved to be extraordinary beyond all expectation. They were golden threads woven in the national fabric. In this, they shamed the political philosophy that discounted their value and rewarded the one that placed its faith in them, thus fulfilling the founding vision of and by and for the people. All its people. (530)

I have memories from when I was a young child of seeing WPA projects in the distance and being told the workers spend all their time leaning on their shovels. I looked hard but did not see anyone doing that, but I believed it just the same.

Out of thousands of such accusations, of course, some were most probably true or half so. It can be difficult at the start getting people who have been out of work into the stride of doing hard, physical labor. It certainly was true for me when, as a child, I worked weeding rows of vegetables on a farm, and later dug ditches for a landscaping firm.

This is an attack not so much on government programs as on Americans laborers depicted as lazy and irresponsible. The result is that disdain stops them from being hired and our country from restoring its crumbling bridges, roads, schools, and infrastructure.

Lloyd Wendt, a reporter for the *Chicago Tribune* in the late 1930s, later became the editor of a Tribune-owned *Chicago's American* newspaper, for which I worked. He loved to tell the story about an assignment he had been given as a young reporter to uncover boondoggling at a WPA construction site in Chicago.

After he reported back to the city desk that he had not observed a single WPA worker lollygagging on the job, the youthful reporter sincerely believed his days as a journalist were over. His specific assignment, he learned, had come via an initialed white piece of paper directly from the Roosevelt and New Deal-hating publisher Colonel Robert R. McCormick. The wrath of Colonel McCormick was legendary, and Wendt felt the note carried with it the implication he had better find what he was told to find—or else!

He did not get fired or even reprimanded. Neither, however, did the positive story he wrote appear in the paper. It did not even show up in Wendt's 861-page book, *The Chicago Tribune: The Rise of a Great American Newspaper* (Rand McNally, 1979). The *Tribune*'s editorials in fact continued to attack on a regular basis "boondoggling" as well as waste and mismanagement on WPA projects.

"After negative stories (on the WPA) had been printed," Wendt acknowledged in his history of the paper, "not much news space remained to deal with the constructive side of the government's program."

The former reporter-turned-author then expanded on what the WPA had done for the infrastructure of the country midway through the WPA's existence:

> By the end of 1936, the historians point out, 1,497 waterworks, 833 sewage treatment plants, 741 street and highway improvements, 263 hospitals, 166 bridges, and 70 municipal power plants had been built, while almost a half billion dollars had been spent on school buildings and $150 million [on] slum clearance.

The current Occupy Wall Street movement has found creative ways to call attention to specific bridges and other structures that require restoration. The most dramatic was the Occupy Boston effort to protest the condition of the Charleston Bridge. The police forbad the demonstrators to march across it lest it collapse!

It is more than bridges and structural damage that need to be sources of employment. A vast panorama of projects today might well parallel what the WPA did in the 1930s. This reality calls for the nation to think bigger, hope more, and charge forward. Modest amount of Obama stimulus money reached out in many directions to do exactly that.

The best trigger for doing this lies in the pages of Nick Taylor's book, *American-Made*:

> WPA workers in Boston had made fish chowder for welfare recipients. New Hampshire's WPA had started a medicinal herb farm where digitalis, lemon balm, peppermint, chamomile, and hyssop were among dozens of plants raised for sale to pharmaceutical companies. In Denver, WPA workers restored fabrics and jewelry found after the death of the notorious "Baby Doe" Tabor, widow of the Leadville, Colorado, mine king Horace Tabor, for display in a museum, thereby burnishing the legend of their affair, silver's boom and bust, and the thirty-five years of impoverished widowhood she spent living in a shack outside Leadville's Matchless Mine, which had given up its riches long before. (330)

We, as inhabitants of this land, stand ready to pass it along to the next generation. In so doing, we face the sobering reality that the country's infrastructure is in trouble. It has been generations since the continent, for the most part, was wired for electricity and colossal projects, including the Hoover Dam, the Golden Gate Bridge, and the interstate highway system were constructed. We are living off an inheritance of steel-and-concrete wonders, grander than anything built by Rome, constructed by "everyday giants" in overalls.

To create jobs, what would be better than
- renewing the transportation system,
- updating and fully staffing our fire and police departments,
- expanding rather than contracting mail service,
- developing jobs and companies that will help the environment,
- investing in safe water supplies, and
- repairing our schools?

Those who argue we cannot afford it are wrong and think like a nation that does not believe in its own future. We cannot be afraid to spend the money to rebuild our crumbling infrastructure. Too many lives, too much of the present, and far too much of our future are at stake.

29

How the Poor Can Be
the Stimulators the Economy Needs

For most of the last century, the basic bargain at the heart of the American economy was that employers paid their workers enough to buy what employers were selling. Unions often negotiated them into doing it.

That basic bargain created a virtuous cycle of higher living standards, more jobs, and better wages.

Back in 1914, Henry Ford announced he was paying workers on his Model T assembly line $5 a day—three times what the typical factory employee earned at the time. The Wall Street Journal termed his action "an economic crime."

But Ford knew it was a cunning business move. The higher wage turned Ford's autoworkers into customers who could afford to buy Model T's. In two years Ford's profits more than doubled.

That was then. Now, Ford Motor Company is paying its new hires half what it paid new employees a few years ago.

The basic bargain is over—not only at Ford but all over the American economy.

—ROBERT B. REICH, CHANCELLOR'S PROFESSOR OF PUBLIC POLICY AT
UC BERKELEY, ON HIS NOVEMBER 28, 2011 BLOG

While filling up at a gas station recently, I was stunned to notice that the last customer to use the pump had purchased exactly $1 worth of gas. It was in a poorer area of Chicago and the price per gallon was hovering around $4, indicating that the individual had purchased one-fourth of a gallon. Over the past few years, I have stood in line at the window of the same station and often observed people asking for $2, $3 or $5 worth of gas, but for me the $1 purchase was a record low.

That $1 was also an indicator of how tight money can be in such a neighborhood. At the fast-food restaurants or corner stores in the area, I see the customers purchasing chicken wings, a plain hamburger, fries, or whatever is the cheapest food item on the menu.

The $1 is also the cost of taking a wildly hopeful gamble by buying a lottery ticket at the corner store. It is not so much supported by logic as a misplaced belief in the notion that things are so bad today that you deserve a little luck. Poverty is often a force that drives people to live in the moment, no matter how foolhardy that may seem to those with reserves.

Yet, a $1 purchase of gas, fast food, or even a lottery ticket can have a more positive impact through stimulating the economy than can a million dollar bonus on which a recipient simply sits.

Many do, without provocation, defy their constraints and buy seemingly unnecessary luxury items such as cigarettes, candy, makeup, beer, and lottery tickets. Such purchases can become symbols of our defiant freedom to do as we please come what may, a protest that just because others think I or you have no right to indulge ourselves, does not make it true.

The poor have so very little, but one thing they do not tend to do is hoard it. The dollar or dime that was in their hands a minute ago is this moment usually being circulated in the economy.

The Institute for Communications Resources March 1, 2008 blog explains the complex principles of economic circulation quite simply: "The global economy today is run like a casino, circulating money from the bottom to the top ... Money is nothing more than a medium of energy exchange that must circulate before it has any wealth-building value."

In our country, the bottom third of the economy equals slightly more than 100 million people. Many, if not most of these, are living day-to-day, if not hour-to-hour, and—when possible—spending accordingly. No such large group of people perhaps in the world circulates money so fast. While each has only small mounts of money, it is a powerful force because of the cumulative amount. Only when we see this multiplied by the number of times the dimes and dollars are turned over can we understand its wealth-creating (and job-creating) impact on the U.S. economy.

This rapid and extensive turnover is a reality that economists understand as basic. Plenty of them do recognize the multiplier effect. The blame is more fairly placed on the mostly Republican members of Congress who reject the view widely held by economists that money placed in the hands of low-income people will provide the biggest boost to the economy because they will spend it the fastest.

Certainly, the money paid as unemployment compensation has done a far better job of helping the economy than the government has by loaning money to banks, which—after distributing bonuses—have for the most part simply deposited the funds into the Federal Reserve Bank. According to the National Inflation Association, banks at the time of this writing have a whopping $1.47 trillion dollars on deposit with the Fed.

The answer is simple and direct: money—preferably that earned through decent-paying jobs but also that distributed through those programs that sustain the poor—helps the overall economy prosper.

This has already been working for this country through such programs as Social Security, the minimum-wage legislation, the G.I. Bill, Medicare, Medicaid, welfare, and the programs of the War on Poverty.

Even the $1 spent at the gas pump for a quarter of a gallon of gas helps sustain the station, pay the salary of the attendant, and reap a tax used to maintain roads. Isolated, it is insignificant; but in an economy that is in need of turnover and aggregate demand, it adds to the plus side of the ledger.

The day laborer, paid minimum wage or less, purchases items at the corner store or from a street vendor. He or she may spend the money within hours of receiving it. The local merchant or vendor may also do so within days. And so may the individuals whom they pay. Each transaction generates an amount of wealth, meets needs, potentially helps create jobs, and stimulates the economy.

Peter Maurin—the cofounder with Dorothy Day of the Catholic Worker House of Hospitality in one of New York's poorest neighborhood—laid out this reality simply. In what he called an "easy essay," he wrote of how putting money into the hands of the poorest of the poor helps stimulate the economy from the bottom up:

> To give money to the poor
>> is to enable the poor to buy.
> To enable the poor to buy
>> is to improve the market.
> To improve the market
>> is to help business.
> To help business
>> is to reduce unemployment.
> To reduce unemployment
>> is to reduce crime.
> To reduce crime
>> is to reduce taxation.

So why not give to the poor
    for business' sake,
    for humanity's sake,
    for God's sake?

Charity also can work to stimulate the economy. Government hand-outs work to stimulate the economy. The entitlement programs of Social Security and Medicare especially help to stimulate it through what they do for people whose incomes have been cut short by retirement, ailments, or age. Government jobs—federal, state, or municipal—stimulate the economy. In the overall picture, they encourage commerce, manufacturing, farming, mining, oil production, health care, the service industry, education, and the general welfare.

The combination of all of the above is what makes our economy function and prosper.

Taxing and spending for national security, for the government to function, to restore the nation's infrastructure, to build roads and improve transportation, to research medical cures, to protect the food and drugs we use, to explore the better use of resources, and to probe space all stimulate the economy and create jobs.

What does not stimulate our economy is to keep money out of the hands of those who will circulate money the fastest.

Public Radio and the Poor

Never belong to any party, always oppose privileged classes and public plunderers, never lack sympathy with the poor, always remain devoted to the public welfare, never be satisfied with merely printing news, always be drastically independent, never be afraid to attack wrong, whether by predatory plutocracy or predatory poverty.
—JOSEPH PULITZER, TO THE 1907 STAFFS OF THE *ST. LOUIS POST DISPATCH* AND THE *NEW YORK WORLD*

Natalie Moore, a reporter for WBEZ 91.5 (Chicago Public Radio), covers what she likes to call "invisible Chicago." She is one of the station's neighborhood bureau reporters, covering the South Side out of the Englewood Bureau.

The neighborhood bureaus date back to 2003 and were a journalistic innovation without parallel or duplication. Rather than shunning poor areas, the radio station placed offices in them.

"We get stories that otherwise would go under the radar," Moore said. "I love it."

She has received recognition for her reporting. The National Association of Black Journalists honored her for a story on the harassment of a transgendered African-American woman who was a resident of Chicago Public Housing. She also received the 2010 Studs Terkel Community Media Award for her work covering the South Side neighborhoods.

Her greatest accomplishment, however, has been enabling Chicagoans to get to know each other and one another's stories, plights, and accomplishments better. The mainstream media covers the courts and crime, religion and politics, business and the arts, but does not pick up on the daily lives, especially of the poor and racial minorities, among over two million Chicago residents. If the media does not have a continuing presence among them, readers, listeners, and TV watchers do not get to meet and understand them other than hearing about crime on their blocks.

WBEZ now has four neighborhood bureaus, including one in nearby Northern Indiana, with several reporters assigned to each.

One of Natalie Moore's stories resulted from her being embedded along with two other reporters in the Robeson High School in Englewood. It allowed her to cover extensively the causes behind the high dropout rate at Robeson and other Chicago-area high schools.

Moore did an extensive story on teenage pregnancy and parenthood, showing that despite efforts by the school to deal with the situation, greater efforts and more resources were needed to be reasonably successful.

Another major story that Chicago Public Radio neighborhood reporters broke was the impact of qualified trauma centers on residents of the city's poorer neighborhoods. "There are Chicagoans," WBEZ reported, "who wonder if trauma care is fair and equal here, too. Right now, none of Chicago's four adult trauma centers is on the South Side."

WBEZ then looked at the situation through the eyes and personal experience of Congressman Bobby Rush (D-IL). The reporter, Natalie Moore, said:

> There are Chicagoans who wonder if trauma care is fair and equal here, too. Right now, none of Chicago's four adult trauma centers is on the South Side. That bothers U.S. Congressman Bobby Rush, who serves a South Side district. For Rush, the issue became personal in 1999.
>
> **RUSH**: My awareness became much more intense when my son was killed right across the street from a hospital.
>
> Rush's son had been shot, and that nearby hospital did not have a trauma center to treat his serious wounds. Instead, Rush's son had to travel from 79th Street to a center at Christ Hospital in south suburban Oak Lawn. The congressman says he feels things could have been different for his son, if the South Side had had its own trauma center.
>
> **RUSH**: He might still be alive today.
>
> Once upon a time, the South Side had several adult trauma centers. Michael Reese and the University of Chicago hospitals each had one.
>
> They eventually closed, leaving a gap on the city's South Side. Rush wants adult trauma care to return, and he's proposed that the federal government fund a center, preferably in his district.
>
> **RUSH**: When you take the whole issue of access to health care in poor, minority and black communities, then it's always not a high priority. It's always too expensive. I just have to say if there weren't a Level I trauma center in a middle-class white communities, there'd be all kind of outcries.

$$\left(\begin{array}{c}31\end{array}\right)$$

Starting from the Bottom Up:
The Key to a Functioning Economy

These unhappy times call for the building of plans ... that build from
the bottom up, and not from the top down, that put their faith once
more in the forgotten man ... the forgotten man at the bottom of the
economic pyramid.
—FRANKLIN DELANO ROOSEVELT, APRIL 7, 1932

Those at the bottom of the economic pyramid often work incredibly hard for very little, with no hope that the situation will ever change. Minimal wages minimize them and cause them to believe it is all they deserve.

And often there is no way out, no comfortable retirement waiting for them, no time off for sickness, much less any real support if they face serious injury or long-term illness.

While they might not have a way out today, they can get a boost a rung or two up the ladder if Congress or their state raises the minimum wage. It is from their perspective that we can see the difference of two or three dollars an hour.

On his September 5, 2011 blog, professor and former Labor Secretary Robert B. Reich (robertreich.org) commented with great insight:

> No economic theories, models or arguments can outweigh the fact that a free and healthy economy depends on the fact that those at or near the bottom of society have a meaningful role as consumers.
>
> Such individuals have very basic needs that include educating children; meeting health needs as well ensuring food, shelter and transportation. They need to be able to earn these, sure, but they also desperately need the incentive to better their lives through adequate, earned wages.
>
> We are not talking simply benevolence or even justice; but most emphatically, a much-needed functioning economy.

A person working full time for a bare minimum wage earns about $15,000 a year, $7,314 less than the poverty level for a family of four. Millions of American workers, because of various legalistic exceptions, are not even protected by the minimum wage laws.

Even the poverty level comparison minimizes the situation, according to David Hilfiker, a physician who has written about poverty. He stated: "An official poverty level that is deceptively low obscures the degree of injustice in the society. It mutes the voices of the poor."

My brother, Paul, a labor economist who mixes his science with common sense and a deep concern for people, has looked into the economics of the minimum wage. He wrote a column, "America Needs a Raise," June 17, 2006 for the *Lebanon Daily News*. The following is an update of that column:

America needs a raise.

Of all the things that have America headed in the wrong direction, one that in the long run is the most serious to the economy and the American way of life, is the erosion of the wages of American workers. If workers can neither maintain their standard of living nor look to a good future for their children, then politics, the environment, and isolated terrorists matter little.

It is, of course, the lowest-wage American workers who need a raise the most. The failure to even keep the minimum wage up with the cost of living drops the bottom out of any other move to increase wages and purchasing power through education or job creation. The adult women in working families who make up most of those affected by the minimum wages are those who would be helped the most.

Had the minimum risen with the cost of living over the past thirty years, it would now be about $10 per hour. Now full-time workers earning the minimum wage of $7.50 an hour receive—before deductions and if they work full time—$15,000 annually. Twice that minimum wage still leaves a family of four eligible for WIC [Women, Infants, and Children] benefits and food stamps.

The legal minimum wage is a conservative Republican's worst nightmare: a law that transfers income to the poor, does it without any tax collection or little administrative cost, and proves that government action can work when markets fail. And labor markets are notorious for their failures.

The central argument against the minimum wage is theoretical: If a market-set wage correctly reflects the productivity of workers, as theory says it should, then setting a floor wage will displace workers. Unfortunately for theory, since 1992 productivity or output per hour in the business sector has risen by 37 percent while unit labor costs and real compensation have risen by only 20 percent. If labor markets worked, wages should also have gone up by 37 percent.

Workers are not getting their fair share because labor markets don't work the way theory says they should. Employers have held the power to overrule theory since the industrial revolution began. Only now, with the crushing of the unions, it is worse.

The usually more practical argument made against a minimum wage is that the increase in costs is too much for small firms to bear. The 1997 increase to $5.15 affected four million workers and increased the wage bill by $741 million. When you add the ripple effect, then it is 15 million workers and $2.0 billion. This is not overwhelming in a $12 trillion economy.

The latest argument is that this ripple effect shoves the whole wage structure up, distorting the wider labor market. If you add the ripple effect to the legally imposed wage increase of 1997, the total cost to the employers was less than 1 percent of the sales revenues of the firms involved. That is, the hotels, fast food, and other low-wage industries would have to raise their prices by 1 percent to cover the cost of that wage increase. This is unlikely to cause job losses.

The federal government may be failing us, but the states are picking up the effort. Eighteen states have minimum wages above the federal level, and about 130 cities and counties have enacted what are called "living-wage" requirements for those with local government contracts. A living wage has many definitions, but it is usually related to the local cost of living and is often set as at 130 percent of the poverty level, well above the federal minimum.

Wages are falling for many reasons: globalization, loss of union bargaining power, and restructuring of the economy being the usual suspects. The problem is that no one is doing anything about it, and the American middle class is lowering its expectations or going into debt that it cannot afford.

The whole economy is suffering, but the working poor are suffering the most, and there is something we can do about it.

If the Republicans and Tea Party followers would just get over their fear and hatred of government, we could raise the minimum wage to $10 an hour and pump money to the people who need it and will spend it.

32

Our "Evolving Standard of Decency"

To none will we sell, to none deny or delay, right or justice.
—*THE MAGNA CARTA*, THE MEADOW AT RUNNYMEDE, JUNE 15, 1215

Despite the miasma of meanness and disdain toward those in need that hovers over parts of the United States, there is hope—and good reason for it. Like a mighty wind, the expansion of human rights has pushed forward for generations as the narrative of our nation.

That wind revealed the rights of the outsider, the underdog, the forgotten, and the disdained, from those without property to former slaves to immigrants to Native Americans to women to the disabled.

Democracy is uniquely under duress now because the top one percent of our nation has gained control of so much of our wealth, and are using the power that goes along with it. The people in the bottom percentiles are finding themselves with fewer rights and less able to participate.

The disproportions at the top and bottom of our economy provide a challenge to our democratic ideals. The Occupy Wall Street movement focuses principally on the top 1 percent of the population having a disproportionate share of America's abundance. They have made this issue central to rectify the desperate poverty that includes one out of three of us at the bottom of the economic scale. Local actions that the movement has taken have included defending people in the process of losing their homes to foreclosure.

Reaching out for fairness and equality is our heritage, and it is who we are called to be in the present and for the future.

We cannot always find the way to a better future solely by going back to the Constitution. We must also look forward to the evolving needs of the country. Abraham Lincoln made this clear in his Cooper Union speech when he said: "I do not mean to say we are bound to follow implicitly in whatever our fathers did [in writing the United States Constitution].

To do so, would be to discard all the lights of current experience—to reject all progress—all improvement."

Our country has a unique record in history for having moved forward in expanding its recognition of individual human rights. While often our nation's pace in doing so has been exceedingly slow and awkward, we eventually respond to those left behind.

In his extraordinarily affirmative book *The People, Yes* (Harcourt Brace and Co., 1936), Carl Sandburg described how we as a nation have moved forward throughout our history:

> The learning and blundering people will live on.
> They will be tricked and sold and again sold
> And go back to the nourishing earth for rootholds,
> > The people so peculiar in renewal and comeback,
> > You can't laugh off their capacity to take it.
> > > The mammoth rests between his cyclonic dramas.

The Supreme Court has given us a fitting term for this positive standard that our nation has maintained. In a major decision, the court called it "the evolving standard of decency that marks the progress of a maturing society."

History books tend to shy away from the words "progress" or "progressives," relegating the terms to a group of early twentieth century liberal dreamers. They sometimes acknowledge people-driven efforts such as abolitionism, the Grange, the suffragette movement, progressive education, the anti-imperialists, the labor movement, civil rights movement.

This long-developing tradition of expanding the concept of human rights is what has awarded our country respect and recognition as a moral nation and a caring people. As Lincoln said in his address dedicating the cemetery at Gettysburg, it began when

> Our fathers brought forth upon this continent a new nation conceived in liberty and dedicated to the proposition that all men are created equal. We are now engaged in a great civil war, testing whether that nation or any nation so conceived and so dedicated can long endure.

This opposition to the continued progress is not new. In the 1890s, Illinois Governor John Peter Altgeld pointed out:

> [Founding father Alexander] Hamilton, speaking for the majority, said, "The people cannot be trusted. You must have great centralized power. You must curb the liberties of the people. Limited

monarchy bottomed on corruption, such as England has, is the best government. Let the government help the rich and trust the rich to help the poor. Hug the shore, follow the customs of the past.

Thomas Jefferson, rather than Hamilton, described the underlying force in our nation as "the latent wisdom of the people." It has been complemented by the United States Supreme Court's legal language for our penchant for progress: "the evolving standard of decency that marks the progress of a maturing society." These words best define the upward staircase we as a nation aspire to ascend.

This key phrase in the history of American jurisprudence best exemplifies our nation's past and hope for progress. The precedent-setting words first came from the pen of Chief Justice Earl B. Warren in a 1958 case, *Tropp v. Dulles*, and were then applied narrowly. Since then, the court has reaffirmed the principle in case after case.

These words—better than any others—acknowledge the growing and developing aspect of democracy. They underline that interpretation that did not hatch as a full-fledged adult in 1787, but has since matured and will continue to do so.

The high court specifically introduced the phrase in *Tropp v. Dulles* as an abiding measure for the Eighth Amendment's clause: "nor shall cruel and unusual punishment be inflicted." For example, on March 1, 2005—in *Roper v. Simmons*—the high court cited these words to bar an individual from the sentence of death for a crime committed as a juvenile (under 18 years of age).

That decision made the United States the last nation in the world to end the execution of those who committed capital crimes as minors. It moved 72 people in 12 states off death row. In writing this decision, Justice Anthony M. Kennedy specifically referred to the high court's "evolving standards of decency" yardstick. These words radiate an evolving moral awareness challenging our nobler and more sensitive selves to understand the meaning of America.

How did the Warren court arrive at these words, "the evolving standards of decency that mark the progress of a maturing society"?

The original case, *Tropp v. Dulles*, involved a man who had been denied a passport because of his one-day desertion during World War II, an act for which he had turned himself in. The issue before the court was whether the subsequent denial of a passport to him represented cruel and unusual punishment.

In rendering the opinion of the court, Chief Justice Warren started by explaining that the phrase "cruel and unusual" was taken directly from the English Declaration of Rights of 1688, and the principle it represented could be traced back to the cornerstone of British law, *The Magna Carta*. Chief Justice Warren continued:

> The basic concept underlying the Eighth Amendment is nothing less than the dignity of man. While the State has the power to punish, the Amendment stands to assure that this power be exercised within the limits of civilized standards.
>
> Fines, imprisonment and even execution may be imposed depending upon the enormity of the crime, but any technique outside the bounds of these traditional penalties is constitutionally suspect. This Court has had little occasion to give precise content to the Eighth Amendment, and, in an enlightened democracy such as ours, this is not surprising. But when the Court was confronted with a punishment of 12 years in irons at hard and painful labor imposed for the crime of falsifying public records, it did not hesitate to declare that the penalty was cruel in its excessiveness and unusual in its character. (Weems v. United States, 217 U.S. 349) The Court recognized in that case that the words of the Amendment are not precise, and that their scope is not static. The Amendment must draw its meaning from the evolving standards of decency that mark the progress of a maturing society.

Similarly understood, the word "decency" in the decision—the dictionary tells us—can be used in its extended sense of nobility and integrity.

Technically, *decency*'s Latin root, *decus,* means what is *fitting*, what is *honorable*, what is of *HUMAN WORTH*.

Our grandchildren and our great-grandchildren will not measure us by our capacity to analyze defeat or an ability to generate brilliant excuses for inaction. Rather, they will do so by how we handle the challenges before us and whether or not we have met them.

The times call for us to believe our destiny is worth achieving, and worth achieving nobly, decently.

Section 5

PRELUDE TO THE FUTURE

The following section of *The Book of the Poor* focuses on the story of poverty here in the United States, what has not worked and what has.

33

Writing Off the Poor
Helped the Confederacy Lose the Civil War

The Confederacy had been built on a very slim foundation of democratic consent. This may have been its greatest weakness.
—STEPHANIE MCCURRY IN HER EPILOGUE TO
CONFEDERATE RECKONING (HARVARD UNIVERSITY PRESS, 2010)

With the words, "promote the general welfare," a government promises its people, "We got your back."

This was the lesson we can learn from the short history of the government that called itself the Confederate States of America.

The story of the Confederacy is a complex one. In addition to slavery and defeat, it was about one section of the American people attempting to break off and form a new nation and scrape together the resources to do so.

Some scholars argue that seceded states' disdain for having the central government accept any responsibility for its citizens implied by the words "promote the general welfare" sealed the fate of Confederacy and, in the end, helped cause its military defeat.

A unique, long-term problem arose from the start because there was no constitutional mandate for the Confederate central government to support or protect the poor and working class under any conditions.

In contrast to the United States Constitution twice using the phrase "to promote the general welfare," the drafters of the Confederate Constitution deliberately omitted the phrase. As a result, the government shockingly neglected the poor and the needy, even the widows and orphans of the soldiers killed in action, as well as the wives and children left behind when men went off to war.

Ultimately, the women left behind first rioted and, as the war wound down, demanded their husbands and sons desert at the very time Lee's army most needed them. This continued even as soldier husbands and fathers died or were maimed on the battlefield. In the end, the unmitigated and unrelieved burden that survivors had to bear helped caused desertions in Robert E. Lee's army and topple the government.

That exclusion has implications today as a fringe, forceful minority seeks to recreate the model of government that helped sink the South.

In drafting their constitution, the Southern secessionists modeled it after the one that the United States forefathers had drafted in 1787.

The Southern breakaway states, in addition to embracing slavery, however, intentionally deleted five of the most significant words that the drafters of the United States Constitution had put in their document.

This phrase, "to promote the general welfare," stands at the center of a government's willingness to insure its citizens. The Confederate government did not say this nor did it do it, although the people very much expected them to help, as the poor and the hundreds of thousands of soldiers' wives and war widows lacked the ability and opportunity to support themselves and their families.

The states-rights-over-all-else politicians did not believe in central government doing anything except electing a president, making war, and creating a legislative body to tax the people to pay for it. They were for less government, which could be achieved only by not making any efforts to promote the welfare of the people. Everything that had to do with their needs and wants, they left for individual states to take care of, if they were willing to do so or could afford it. And, most decidedly, the central government as well as the Constitution made it clear that it was not the responsibility of the Confederacy to ascertain, help, or make certain the states had the people's backs.

To them, states rights were important; personal ones, far less so.

The South did not even have a Supreme Court to recognize, establish personal rights, or enforce them.

Most certainly, the Confederacy did not and never would embrace the Preamble to the Declaration of Independence, which states:

> We hold these truths to be self-evident, that all men are created equal, that they are endowed by their Creator with certain unalienable Rights, that among these are Life, Liberty and the pursuit of Happiness. That to secure these rights, Governments are instituted among Men, deriving their just powers from the consent of the governed—That whenever any Form of Government becomes destructive of these ends, it is the Right of the People to alter or to abolish it, and to institute new Government, laying its foundation

on such principles and organizing its powers in such form, as to them shall seem most likely to effect their Safety and Happiness.

The results of a supposedly democratic government not putting "to promote the general welfare" at the very top level of its priorities proved to be a disastrous omission for the South.

During the war, it was not as they feared—the slaves rebelling—but rather the "defection" of the poor, hungry and non-slave-owning women who saw their husbands and sons go off to battle for the South.

Those historians who have bothered to look at what was happening on the home front in the Confederacy tend to agree with Bell Irvin Wiley, who stated in his book *The Plain People of the Confederacy* (Louisiana University Press, 1944): "Long before the finale at Appomattox, the doom of the Confederacy had been firmly sealed by the wide-spread defection of its humblest subjects."

Stephanie McCurry in her scholarly *Confederate Reckoning* (Harvard College, 2010) is even more specific:

> When the C.S.A. [Confederate States of America] adopted a draft of white men, when it enlisted 85 percent of adult white men and stripped the countryside of labor, when it attempted to create a tax base and supply the army by a levy on the "surplus" agricultural production of farms and plantations, it extracted the means of war from a population of women and children staggering under the burden of farm labor and, by 1863, facing starvation. (359)

Simply put, the poor whites—led by, of all people, their women—protested and then, when the pleas failed, in 1863 started rioting in city after city. Finally, and most effectively, they convinced their sons and husbands to abandon even Lee's dwindling army.

Individual states—at least a few of them—tried to meet the needs of soldiers' wives and widows.

Within a year after the war began, the letters started. In poorly written and often misspelled missives, the suffering poor women of the South often signed themselves by adding "sw" for soldier's wife. They desperately pleaded for food and clothing. These initially were addressed to President Jefferson Davis or the federal government. When they went unanswered, the women turned to their state governments.

Their most basic request was that their drafted husbands and sons be allowed to return home to plant the crops or harvest them. They were especially angry that individuals who owned 20 or more slaves were exempt from the draft. Theoretically, this exemption was made so the individual could help in stopping the slaves from rioting or running away.

Often the letters they wrote before rioting were uniquely poignant because even the spelling in them spoke of the women's frustration and powerlessness.

One woman wrote to Govenor Zebulon Vance of North Carolina:

> i want you if you plese you and Mr Davis to fix preperashenes (preparations) to send home poer solgers to cut the wheat for we have soad (sowed) about fiftween bushel ... excepten you fixes sum way fer ous we can not get it ous ... i hope that you and Mr Davis will helpe ous all you can fer all the wones that can dew aney thing.

She understood who had to act. A woman at the bottom of the pile was calling Confederate President Jefferson Davis to assume a role that he had deliberately refused for himself and his central government, a refusal that would lead to a measurably extent to the defeat of the Confederacy.

By 1863, when their letters of protest had not worked, women brazenly broke into stores to take food or other necessities. During the "bread riots," as they were called, large groups in cities small and large throughout the South armed themselves. Using hatchets, knives, and guns, they broke into store after store and seized food and clothing. Often, they left behind what little Confederate money they did have in order to pay what they could for what they had taken.

Many of the rioters were war widows and women who had lost their sons in the conflict or had seen them maimed and unable to help their families earn a living. Nevertheless, to the very end, Jefferson Davis and the Confederate government refused to provide for the welfare of the people.

The Southern women who subsequently rioted in cities such as Mobile, Atlanta, and Richmond directly challenged the structure. Some of them went to jail, with one given a five-year sentence. Still, they provided the country with a lesson in realpolitik a century before the feminist movement took hold. The message given was that, if the government abandons the responsibility for the general welfare, then those who are repressed can and will stand up.

They did get responses. Many states attempted to help them out; but, in almost every instance, the individual states did not have the resources or even the legal power to get soldiers excused from the military in even the most dire situations.

During the Civil War, however, the South lost a quarter of its soldiers, over 100,000 men—husbands, fathers, brothers, and single men. Many of these were very poor when recruited or drafted and left behind wives, children, families, and relatives even more destitute as a result of their injuries and deaths. As the war went on, their numbers multiplied and the resources available to those left behind became fewer.

By the end of the war, wives had turned to pleading with their soldier husbands and sons to desert and come home to help them with the crops, even though desertion could mean a firing squad.

Shelby Foote, in his *The Civil War: A Narrative*, showed the astounding dimension of the desertion problem. When Robert E. Lee and his troops were making their last stand in the trenches at Petersburg, Virginia, Foote reports that a total of 198,494 Confederate soldiers were listed as "absent from the Confederate ranks." On the same day, the total number of gray-clad soldier in all theaters of action "present for action" was only 125,994.

No one could win a war that way.

The denial of the government's responsibility "to care for the general welfare" has significant implications today. A forceful, fringe minority is trying to recreate the model of that government—to subtract "promote the general welfare" from the national understanding of the Constitution. That approach, 150 years ago, helped sink the Confederacy.

Our nation has a history of marches, protests, and riots; but none of these actions was so clearly focused on the idea of the insuring the general welfare, as was the effort to encourage the men of the South to desert.

The general welfare clause has a long history and a pressing one today as lowering the debt is being given a higher precedence over the general welfare of the people of this country.

Documents stating the government has a responsibility for the welfare of the people go back to 1637. In that year, Govenor John Winthrop of the Massachusetts Bay Company wrote that the essential form of a body politic should be "the consent of a certain company of people to cohabitate [*sic*] together under one government for their mutual safety and welfare."

This core American idea is found also in the Articles of Confederation, Virginia's constitution, and the United States Constitution in the words "the general welfare." That came in the second reference to "the general welfare" in the United States Constitution (Article I, Section 8) and gave Congress the power to raise funds and spend them on insuring the general welfare. It is the issue today that cannot be erased, as it was in the short life of the Confederacy.

In his second inaugural address, President Franklin Delano Roosevelt took the common or general welfare cause from a promising bud to a blooming flower. After he had said, "I see one-third of a nation ill-housed, ill-clad, ill-nourished," he added:

> We of the Republic sensed the truth that democratic government has innate capacity to protect its people against disasters once considered inevitable, to solve problems once considered unsolvable. We would not admit that we could not find a way to master economic epidemics just as, after centuries of fatalistic suffering, we had found a way to master epidemics of disease. We refused to leave the problems of our common welfare to be solved by the winds of chance and the hurricanes of disaster.
>
> In this we Americans were discovering no wholly new truth; we were writing a new chapter in our book of self-government.

It was a chapter the Confederacy refused to write from which arch-conservatives could learn today.

34

FDR's "The Forgotten Man" Address

April 7, 1932
(EXCERPTS)

Although I understand that I am talking under the auspices of the Democratic National Committee, I do not want to limit myself to politics. I do not want to feel that I am addressing an audience of Democrats or that I speak merely as a Democrat myself. The present condition of our national affairs is too serious to be viewed through partisan eyes for partisan purposes.

Fifteen years ago my public duty called me to an active part in a great national emergency, the World War. Success then was due to a leadership whose vision carried beyond the timorous and futile gesture of sending a tiny army of 150,000 trained soldiers and the regular navy to the aid of our allies. The generalship of that moment conceived of a whole Nation mobilized for war, economic, industrial, social and military resources gathered into a vast unit capable of and actually in the process of throwing into the scales ten million men equipped with physical needs and sustained by the realization that behind them were the united efforts of 110,000,000 human beings. It was a great plan because it was built from bottom to top and not from top to bottom.

In my calm judgment, the Nation faces today a more grave emergency than in 1917.

It is said that Napoleon lost the battle of Waterloo because he forgot his infantry—he staked too much upon the more spectacular but less substantial cavalry. The present administration in Washington provides a close parallel. It has either forgotten or it does not want to remember the infantry of our economic army.

These unhappy times call for the building of plans that rest upon the forgotten, the unorganized but the indispensable units of economic power, for plans like those of 1917 that build from the bottom up and not from the top down, that put their faith once more in the forgotten man at the bottom of the economic pyramid.

Obviously, these few minutes tonight permit no opportunity to lay down the ten or a dozen closely related objectives of a plan to meet our present emergency, but I can draw a few essentials, a beginning in fact, of a planned program.

It is the habit of the unthinking to turn in times like this to the illusions of economic magic. People suggest that a huge expenditure of public funds by the Federal Government and by State and local governments will completely solve the unemployment problem. But it is clear that even if we could raise many billions of dollars and find definitely useful public works to spend these billions on, even all that money would not give employment to the seven million or ten million people who are out of work. Let us admit frankly that it would be only a stopgap. A real economic cure must go to the killing of the bacteria in the system rather than to the treatment of external symptoms.

How much do the shallow thinkers realize, for example, that approximately one-half of our whole population, fifty or sixty million people, earn their living by farming or in small towns whose existence immediately depends on farms. They have today lost their purchasing power. Why? They are receiving for farm products less than the cost to them of growing these farm products. The result of this loss of purchasing power is that many other millions of people engaged in industry in the cities cannot sell industrial products to the farming half of the Nation. This brings home to every city worker that his own employment is directly tied up with the farmer's dollar. No Nation can long endure half bankrupt. Main Street, Broadway, the mills, the mines will close if half the buyers are broke.

I cannot escape the conclusion that one of the essential parts of a national program of restoration must be to restore purchasing power to the farming half of the country. Without this the wheels of railroads and of factories will not turn.

Closely associated with this first objective is the problem of keeping the homeowner and the farm-owner where he is, without being dispossessed through the foreclosure of his mortgage. His relationship to the great banks of Chicago and New York is pretty remote. The two billion dollar fund which President Hoover and the Congress have put at the disposal of the big banks, the railroads and the corporations of the Nation is not for him.

His is a relationship to his little local bank or local loan company. It is a sad fact that even though the local lender in many cases does not want to evict the farmer or home-owner by foreclosure proceedings, he is forced to do so in order to keep his bank or company solvent. Here should be an objective of Government itself, to provide at least as much assistance to the little fellow as it is now giving to the large banks and corporations. That is another example of building from the bottom up.

One other objective closely related to the problem of selling American products is to provide a tariff policy based upon economic common sense rather than upon politics, hot-air, and pull. This country during the past few years, culminating with the Hawley-Smoot Tariff in 1929, has compelled the world to build tariff fences so high that world trade is decreasing to the vanishing point. The value of goods internationally exchanged is today less than half of what it was three or four years ago.

Every man and woman who gives any thought to the subject knows that if our factories run even 80 percent of capacity, they will turn out more products than we as a Nation can possibly use ourselves. The answer is that if they run on 80 percent of capacity, we must sell some goods abroad. How can we do that if the outside Nations cannot pay us in cash? And we know by sad experience that they cannot do that. The only way they can pay us is in their own goods or raw materials, but this foolish tariff of ours makes that impossible.

What we must do is this: revise our tariff on the basis of a reciprocal exchange of goods, allowing other Nations to buy and to pay for our goods by sending us such of their goods as will not seriously throw any of our industries out of balance, and incidentally making impossible the continuance of pure monopolies which cause us to pay excessive prices for many of the necessities of life.

Such objectives as these three, restoring farmers' buying power, relief to the small banks and homeowners and a reconstructed tariff policy, are only a part of ten or a dozen vital factors. But they seem to be beyond the concern of a national administration, which can think in terms only of the top of the social and economic structure. It has sought temporary relief from the top down rather than permanent relief from the bottom up. It has totally failed to plan ahead in a comprehensive way. It has waited until something has cracked and then at the last moment has sought to prevent total collapse.

It is high time to get back to fundamentals. It is high time to admit with courage that we are in the midst of an emergency at least equal to that of war. Let us mobilize to meet it.

35

Thank You, Depression-Era Generation

A national political movement came to power in the 1930s. Its antecedents went back to the end of the nineteenth century. The movement, which took its name from a phrase used by Franklin Delano Roosevelt—the New Deal—was not limited to the actions of Roosevelt and his political party; it extended far deeper into the ethics, politics, religion, and aesthetics of the country.
—EARL SHORRIS, *THE POLITICS OF HEAVEN*

"Things will get better," our parents encouraged us, their children, during the Great Depression of the 1930s. It represented their belief—sometimes only tentatively held—but urged upon us to make it our own.

The optimism and encouragement, which they espoused, relied heavily on their making a significant effort to help bring about what they promised.

Such hopeful conviction, they believed, would override for us kids the rampant dire economic predictions and discouraging analysis that seemed to be everywhere and in everything. They put heart and soul into making things be better.

Little did they realize that the changes they were bringing about would last for generations and be there for their grandchildren as well.

My mother, despite raising six young children during the 1930s, worked at night in the at-home cottage industry making wood fiber flowers. My father was fortunate enough to have a job at Chevrolet Gear and Axle, even if it was only for two days a week. On the other days, he went door to door selling a wall-cleaning compound he had mixed.

My mother and father, as so many parents do today, were trying to use the arrows of their self-sacrifices to mitigate the hardships that we their children were encountering.

To me, the adults of Great Depression tried to push hope and optimism to overcome discouragement and despair.

John Coyne, 81 years old, remembers the Depression for the printers' union commitment to helping save his family. His father was a printer in Chicago, and, in the 1930s, there was very little work for anyone in the trade. Supported by their members, however, union leaders set up a plan to spread out what work was available so that every printer would get at least two days work a month.

"It was not easy," Coyne recalled. "Still, we were at least able to survive on what my father earned." It was a different world. Parents had their ways of doing the best they could in the Depression. It still goes on today with the poor. I recall a desperately discouraged mother who was on welfare telling me with sadness and pride:

> Last year, I had $7 to buy Christmas with. That didn't include any money to buy a tree. I bought my daughter mittens. The little ones, I got each a small truck from the dime store. The two big ones got 79-cent rockets you could shoot up in the air. I was able to buy a little candy and some nuts. That was it.

In human terms, the Depression urge to sprinkle hope in a child's life is encapsulated in the following passage from John Steinbeck's 1939 book, *The Grapes of Wrath*.

The novel starts with the poor Oklahoman dirt farmers journeying westward to escape the dustbowl and to look for jobs in the orchards of farm fields and vineyards of California. It includes the following poignant incident:

> "May sound funny to be so tight," he apologized. "We got a thousan' miles to go, an' we don' know if we'll make it." He dug into the pouch with a forefinger, located a dime, and pinched in for it. When he put it down on the counter he had a penny with it. He was about to drop the penny back into the pouch when his eye fell on the two boys frozen before the candy counter. He moved slowly down to them. He pointed in the case at the big long strips of peppermint. "Is them penny candy, ma'am?"
>
> Mae moved down and looked in. "Which ones?"
>
> "There, them stripy ones."
>
> The little boys raised their eyes to her face and they stopped breathing; their mouths were partly open, their half-baked bodies were rigid.
>
> "Oh—them. Well, no—them's two for a penny."

In the story, it turned out, they were regularly "nickel apiece candy," but the boys got them for the made-up cheaper price.

I am a child of the Depression. I was about the same age those two boys were in 1939. I experienced over and over again the kind of generosity that was exhibited in that fictional incident. My parents found ways to give us little treats and to remind us that indeed, "Things will get better." Others went out of their way to be kind also.

At the same time, they and their generation worked very hard for it to happen not just for us but also for others and for future generations.

They wanted not only opportunity for us to compete more successfully in the world around but also for the pie to be cut in bigger pieces for the rest of the people as well as their children. They willingly showed the spirit of sacrifice that a generation must have to help democracy become a meaningful word.

While a sadness all but overwhelms me to see the contrast with the 1930s in the apparent selfishness today of so many loud and vocal Americans, I also perceive with excitement the Occupy Movement returning the nation to a shared caring spirit like that of the 1930s.

Such an effort in the Depression era did work out. Things did get better and, as we grew up, we kept the memory of our parents' pledge in front of us.

In retrospect, we both value and take for granted what their generation, led by President Franklin Delano Roosevelt, accomplished. It established a structure of targeted programs that ultimately gave us by right a fairer and bigger share of America's abundance.

I have felt a generational pride in the improved forests, the electrification, bridge, infrastructure additions, and parks and local community projects such as local libraries, post offices, and municipal buildings that the WPA and Civilian Conservation Corps contributed to America.

What a heritage we had been handed and have enjoyed all our lives!

As a child in 1939, I witnessed exciting new symbols of "things getting better."

The beginning of the fulfillment of my parents' promise came into my life not in the form of a mouthwatering peppermint stick as in *The Grapes of Wrath*; but through the introduction of bright colors, portending a life I had not known existed.

Color—along with my parents' growing confidence in what they could afford us—announced to me, "Everything would be different; it would be better."

As color entered my world, I began to experience small, new celebrations of happiness, a quicker pace and new texture to life. There were extra little treats, more frequent smiles, larger portions of food, and less frequently my father needing to say "like it or lump it" about the leftovers on our plates.

This is the discovery—this blossoming of color and of hope—which we can want for the poor children of this nation and the world.

For my generation, a change really happened.

My parents and their generation helped it come about because they knew that better times could come only if things changed for others, and had opportunity, too.

The Depression generation gave me hope, brought color into my life, and left behind the network of social service programs that created, for my generation, that first big step upward out of want.

We did not know or understand it, but we were gaining entry into the middle class and would retain our membership all our lives.

The price of coming together as a caring nation would be enormous for many adults, and they paid it ungrudgingly. It would be the lives and limbs of their children sacrificed to defeat the forces that wanted to take away our democracy, destroy the Jews as a people, and put an end to our sacred belief in equality.

Yet, there are people today who selfishly seek to weaken the entitlement programs, eliminate the help that food stamps bring to the hungry, and cut off labor unions that have for generations had the backs of American workers. These individuals demand health care be not available to all and look askance at solutions they themselves had previously proposed, such as hiring the unemployed to restore this nation's infrastructure.

In their small-mindedness and lack of concern for others, these individuals are totally out of tune with the generosity and concern their grandparents and great-grandparents had in developing an effective American social conscience. In so doing, they are shortsighted, and seem nothing less than mean-spirited.

The Depression-era generation used ingenuity, forethought, concern for others, determination, political action, and new ideas to fashion safe passage for so many of them along the way into the middle class.

They were not overly ambitious. They did not want streets paved with gold, but they wanted paved streets. They did not want fortunes; they wanted jobs at which they could work hard and which, in turn, provided security for their families. They did not want wings with which to fly to the top of the heap; they wanted a ladder of educational opportunity for their sons and daughters to be able to climb up out of their troubles. And they succeeded. Look at us.

To get to that dream of the middle class required large numbers with government help to pull themselves up together so they could produce goods and, after the war, acquire homes, household appliances, and cars. This they did, but they also created suburbs, built schools, founded churches, and reached out with the Marshall Plan to save Europe. Doing so generated jobs for each other.

In the Depression these opportunities all seemed so far off in the future that we needed a metaphor such as color to assure us things could be different. I know I did.

Our nitty-gritty world reflected the ashen soot of our basement coal furnaces; the thin gray layers falling gently from the smoke-belching factories in Detroit; the noisy, coal-and-oil-burning locomotives of the Grand Trunk Railroad at the end of our block. But we did manage to experience happiness, hope, and laughter.

Our clothes had been hand-ironed, hand-scrubbed, handsewn and handed down. Girls' dresses were pale, flour-sack hues. To clean these clothes, mothers had to rely on muscle power and a corrugated metal scrubboard. Their toughened hands lost their youth and texture to their amateurishly crafted soap made from lye and table fats.

On the west side of our small rented house was a trellis rich with dozens and dozens of roses. These furnished a delightful aroma, one that roses no longer seem to possess. The soot from the coal-burning furnaces and nearby railroad engines, however, quickly dulled their sheen, as it did everything else.

My mother's face and those of her friends told the story of the Depression. No powder touched up the soft circles of darkness under their eyes. "We can't afford it," I heard my mother tell a clerk who tried to sell her makeup.

Sharing and sacrifice were big factors in people's lives. My uncle Harry and aunt Rhea owned an orchard ten miles from our home, and they allowed our family—kids and all—to pick as many apples as we could. We took home bushels of apples on the car fenders, trunk, and roof to eat, sell, and share with our neighbors.

A good third of the families on our block took in—as we did—an elderly relative. In our case, it was Aunt Ella. We had little room and even less money to afford to do it; but we, like our neighbors, did it anyway.

When they knocked, door-to-door sales people often got something. Even if a homeowner (or renter) could not afford to buy anything from them, there would be an offer of a glass of water, a few seconds of listening, a "good luck," or a referral to someone further down the block.

Like the poor everywhere, the people of the Depression learned through experience that sharing represented what was best about our nation. They left behind a living blueprint for how looking out for one another had the power to revitalize the American dream. It included a sense of sharing with which the Depression generation inspired the next two generations to provide the Marshall Plan and the War on Poverty.

Have we as a nation started to lose that experience of sharing and the hope it brought with it?

36

An Economic Bill of Rights

In our personal ambitions we are individualists. But in our seeking for economic and political progress as a nation, we all go up or else all go down as one people.
—PRESIDENT FRANKLIN DELANO ROOSEVELT

It was January 11, 1944. The D-day landings in France were still five months off, and the outcome of World War II was yet in the balance.

The president of the United States, Franklin Delano Roosevelt, considered what promise, what kind of pledge he could make that would show people what kind of a future they were sending their fathers, sons, and brothers to fight and die for.

The answer came in a document spelling out the rights and the hopes of citizens—just as it had ultimately done in the founding of our nation. After the American Revolution, the government clarified for its people their political rights in the Constitution and then in the Bill of Rights.

President Roosevelt's effort—an intense one to portray what the future should look like—was a visionary blueprint for a nation learning from sacrifice and tragedy. What he sought to formulate was a message worthy to be a follow-up to those heart-tugging government telegrams that began, "We regret to inform you ..."

His State of the Union message outlined a program to jump-start the American people toward a better, fairer world for those in want, just as the state of our country calls for such a vision today.

He wanted to hand people not just a slice of the nation's abundance but also the right to earn it. Roosevelt's statement—like Abraham Lincoln's Gettysburg Address and Emancipation Proclamation—was in the midst of war and was in furtherance of our nation understanding and accepting basic human rights as the highway to care for all its citizens. We have Roosevelt's words. They are monumental. We can no longer leave them on the shelf.

His speech told the Congress and the country:

> This republic had its beginning, and grew to its present strength under the protection of certain inalienable political rights—among them the right of free speech, free press, free worship, trial by jury, freedom from unreasonable searches and seizures. They were our rights to life and liberty. As our nation has grown in size and stature, however—as our industrial economy expanded—these political rights proved inadequate in the pursuit of happiness. ...
>
> We have accepted, so to speak, a second Bill of Rights, under which a new basis of security and prosperity can be established for all—regardless of station, race, or creed.

His specifics included the following:

> The right to a useful and remunerative job in the industries or shops or farms or mines of the nation;
>
> The right to earn enough to provide adequate food and clothing and recreation;
>
> The right of every farmer to raise and sell his products at a return, which will give him and his family a decent living;
>
> The right of every businessman, large and small, to trade in an atmosphere of freedom from unfair competition and domination by monopolies at home or abroad;
>
> The right of every family to a decent home;
>
> The right to adequate medical care and the opportunity to achieve and enjoy good health;
>
> The right to adequate protection from the economic fears of old age, sickness, accident and unemployment;
>
> The right to a good education.
>
> All of these rights spell security. And after the war is won, we must be prepared to move forward, in the implementation of these rights, to new goals of human happiness and well-being.

Out of respect and appreciation for what they had done for their country, he offered America a new sense of our rights and the opportunity to enjoy a better life than what the Depression had afforded them.

President Roosevelt was making a promise to the generation waging the war—a future that would not be a repeat of the 1930s with their day-to-day unfair gaps in jobs, wages, farm policies, education, and medical care.

This "Second Bill of Rights" he offered was more than a pledge. When he added that "our fighting men abroad—and their families at home—

expect such a program and have a right to insist upon it," he was proposing his list of economic rights as a war memorial.

He signed the first part of his pledge—given directly to those who served in the military—into law on June 22, 1944. Congress labeled it as the Servicemen's Readjustment Act of 1944, but it became better known as the G.I. Bill of Rights. That law invested billions of American dollars in education and job training for millions of veterans and helped enormous numbers of them get loans to afford housing.

Although President Lyndon Johnson did not refer to Roosevelt, he did not propose the late President's legislative agenda as an economic bill of rights, but that is what it was. And by 1965, the Congress of the United States enacted a major portion of Roosevelt's "Second Bill of Rights" pledge into law as Johnson's "the Great Society" program.

The focus was not on World War II and the soldiers who served in it, but on the people left behind in not sharing in the nation's abundance. Roosevelt had outlined a new sense of rights and promised America that the government would make good for them.

Twenty years later, Johnson carried through on it. The Great Society programs included

- the Civil Rights Act of 1964, and its promises of equality toward those who had been denied it;
- Medicare, a bedrock health insurance program for the elderly;
- Medicaid, a program providing health care assistance for the poor;
- Head Start for preschool children of those with limited economic advantage, and federal aid for education given to states based on the number of their children from low-income families;
- the Department of Housing and Urban Development, to open opportunity for decent housing to those whose families could not otherwise afford it;
- Volunteers in Service to America (VISTA), whose members worked in the Appalachian region, migrant worker camps in California, and poor neighborhoods, and started agricultural cooperatives, community groups, and small businesses that still thrive today;
- the Job Corps;
- Community Development Block Grants, offering shared local and federal help for impoverished areas; and
- the Office of Economic Opportunity, which provided training for the poor and established various community-action programs providing the poor themselves a voice in housing, health, and education programs.

America benefited as a result.

A groundswell of financial aid and voluntarism produced a moral revolution, which most of the nation applauded and with which they found ways to become involved.

Between 1965 and 1968, because of the War on Poverty, the Civil Rights Act, and a spike in the economy, the income of black families rose from 54 to 60 percent of that of white families.

During those years, across the board—not just at the top—wages and opportunity increased.

37

Initiating a War Against Poverty

*The following excerpt is from President Johnson's message to
Congress that initiated the War on Poverty. It is real, specific,
and truly belongs in American visionary literature alongside
Dr. Martin Luther King Jr.'s "I Have a Dream" speech.*

From Lyndon B. Johnson's Message to Congress, March 16, 1964

We are citizens of the richest and most fortunate country in the history of the world. One hundred and eighty years ago we were a small country struggling for survival on the margin of a great land. Today we have established a civilization of freemen which spans an entire continent.

With the growth of our country has come opportunity for our people—opportunity to educate our children, to use our energies in productive work, to increase our leisure—opportunity for almost every American to hope through work and talent he could create a better life for himself and his family.

The path has not always been an easy one. But we have never lost sight of our goal—an America in which every citizen shares all the opportunities of his society, in which every man has a chance to advance his welfare to the limit of his capacities. We have come a long way toward this goal. We still have a long way to go.

The distance which remains is the measure of the great unfinished work of our society. To finish that work I have called for a national war on poverty. Our objective: total victory.

There are millions of Americans—one-fifth of our people—who have not shared in the abundance which has been granted to most of us, and on whom the gates of opportunity have been closed. What does this poverty mean to those who endure it? It means a daily struggle to secure the necessities for even a meager existence. It means that the abundance, the comforts, the opportunities they see all around them are beyond their grasp. Worst of all, it means hopelessness for the young.

The young man or woman who grows up without a decent education, in a broken home, in a hostile and squalid environment in ill health or in the face of racial injustice—that young man or woman is often trapped in a life of poverty. He does not have the skills demanded by a complex society. He does not know how to acquire these skills. He faces a mounting sense of despair, which drains initiative and ambition and energy. ...

This is only part of the story. Our history has proved that each time we broaden the base of abundance, giving more people the chance to produce and consume, we create new industry, higher production, increased earnings, and better income for all. Giving new opportunity to those who have little will enrich the lives of the rest.

Because it is right, because it is wise, and because, for the first time in our history, it is possible to conquer poverty, I submit, for the consideration of the Congress and the country, the Economic Opportunity Act of 1964.

The Act does not merely expand old programs or improve what is already being done. It charts a new course. It strikes at the causes, not just the consequences of poverty. It can be a milestone in our 180-year search for a better life for our people.

This Act provides five basic opportunities. It will give almost half a million underprivileged young Americans the opportunity to develop skills, continue education, and find useful work. It will give every American community the opportunity to develop a comprehensive plan to fight its own poverty and help them to carry out their plans. It will give dedicated Americans the opportunity to enlist as volunteers in the war against poverty. It will give many workers and farmers the opportunity to break through particular barriers which bar their escape from poverty. It will give the entire nation the opportunity for a concerted attack on poverty through the establishment, under my direction, of the Office of Economic Opportunity, a national headquarters for the war against poverty.

This is how we propose to create these opportunities.

First we will give high priority to helping young Americans who lack skills, who have not completed their education or who cannot complete it because they are too poor. The years of high school and college are the most critical of a young person's life. If they are not helped then, many will be condemned to a life of poverty which they, in turn, will pass on to their children.

I therefore recommend the creation of a Job Corps, a Work-Training Program, and a Work Study Program. A new national Job Corps will build toward an enlistment of 100,000 young men. They will be drawn from those whose background, health and education make them least fit for useful work ...

Half of these young men will work, in the first year, on special conservation projects to give them education, useful work experience and to enrich the natural resources of the country.

Half of these young men will receive, in the first year, a blend of training, basic education and work experience in job Training Centers ...

A new national Work-Training Program operated by the Department of Labor will provide work and training for 200,000 American men and women between the ages of 16 and 21. This will be developed through state and local governments and nonprofit agencies. ...

A new national Work-Study Program operated by the Department of Health, Education, and Welfare will provide federal funds for part-time jobs for 140,000 young Americans who do not go to college because they cannot afford it.

There is no more senseless waste than the waste of the brainpower and skill of those who are kept from college by economic circumstance. Under this program they will, in a great American tradition, be able to work their way through school ...

Second, through a new Community Action program we intend to strike at poverty at its source—in the streets of our cities and on the farms of our countryside among the very young and the impoverished old.

This program asks men and women throughout the country to prepare long-range plans for the attack on poverty in their own local communities. ...

Third, I ask for the authority to recruit and train skilled volunteers for the war against poverty. Thousands of Americans have volunteered to serve the needs of other lands. Thousands more want the chance to serve the needs of their own land. They should have that chance.

Among older people who have retired, as well as among the young, among women as well as men, there are many Americans who are ready to enlist in our war against poverty.

They have skills and dedication. They are badly needed. ...

Fourth, we intend to create new opportunities for certain hard-hit groups to break out of the pattern of poverty.

Through a new program of loans and guarantees we can provide incentives to those who will employ the unemployed.

Through programs of work and retraining for unemployed fathers and mothers we can help them support their families in dignity while preparing themselves for new work.

Through funds to purchase needed land, organize cooperatives, and create new and adequate family farms we can help those whose life on the land has been a struggle without hope.

Fifth, I do not intend that the war against poverty become a series of uncoordinated and unrelated efforts—that it perish for lack of leadership and direction.

Therefore this bill creates, in the Executive Office of the President, a new Office of Economic Opportunity. Its Director will be my personal Chief of Staff for the War against poverty. I intend to appoint Sargent Shriver to this post. ...

What you are being asked to consider is not a simple or an easy program. But poverty is not a simple or an easy enemy.

It cannot be driven from the land by a single attack on a single front. Were this so, we would have conquered poverty long ago.

Nor can it be conquered by government alone ...

Today, for the first time in our history, we have the power to strike away the barriers to full participation in our society. Having the power, we have the duty ...

It (the War on Poverty) will provide a lever with which we can begin to open the door to our prosperity for those who have been kept outside.

It will also give us the chance to test our weapons, to try our energy and ideas and imagination for the many battles yet to come. As conditions change, and as experience illuminates our difficulties, we will be prepared to modify our strategy.

And this program is much more than a beginning.

Rather it is a commitment. It is a total commitment by this President, and this Congress, and this nation, to pursue victory over the most ancient of mankind's enemies.

$$38$$

Victory in the War on Poverty

These years deserve a more discriminating verdict.
—MICHAEL B. KATZ, *THE UNDESERVING POOR: FROM THE WAR ON POVERTY TO THE WAR ON WELFARE*

More than 12,000,000 people were freed from destitution in the first five years of the War on Poverty (1965–1969), establishing that an all-out attack on poverty can succeed.

The number of Americans living below the poverty threshold during those years dropped from 36,000,000 to 24,000,000.

Because of the economic stimulation that occurred among the very poor, the economy started functioning better from the bottom up. It helped America increase wages and profits, paid for the War, contributed to the cost of the moon landing, and funded the war in Vietnam.

Despite this upturn in the economy from stages where stimulus did not traditionally come, many have written off the impact of the War on Poverty on the quality of life of poor people in this country. They argue that it was an upswing in the economy that generated the jobs that saved the millions of Americans in those years.

The Republican Congress of the 1980s and even many liberals since then have adopted President Reagan's final but false verdict: "We fought a war on poverty. Poverty won."

Milton Friedman—the high priest of conservative economics—supported Reagan's biased conclusion as strongly as anyone. He, along with Republicans in Congress, used the president's words as an obituary for the War on Poverty and as proof that government should not come to the assistance of the poor. Friedman added what his followers considered the *coup de grace* to the great American social economic endeavor, the War on Poverty. He asserted that, because of their interventionist nature, Lyndon Johnson's policies actually had a negative impact on the economy.

In fact, the economy surged to a great extent precisely because of the War on Poverty. It was a successfully targeted stimulus that mirrored what the New Deal programs had done for the economy during the Depression. Poor people got government-sponsored benefits—training and jobs that, in turn, created more jobs and a spiraling flow of cash benefits, money in people's pockets while it also paid for essential services. By becoming more relevant consumers and producers, even the formerly long-term unemployed and unemployable were able to stimulate the economy and help cause and continue the upswing.

An earlier upswing in 1964 assisted those most easy and ready to be helped, as is usual at the end of a recession or depression, but then the figures tend to slow down as the long-term unemployed struggle to reintegrate into the economy. Still, the figures show that the War on Poverty reached even them.

In calling for a War on Poverty, President Johnson had both warned and prophesized:

> We are fully aware that this program will not eliminate all the poverty in America in a few months or a few years. Poverty is deeply rooted and its causes are many. But this program will show the way to new opportunities for millions of our fellow citizens.

When we look into the lives of real people at that point, we realize better the particulars of how deep-rooted poverty was, how much there was to do and why.

Interviews with two poor Chicago mothers on public aid in early 1965 illustrate that story. The following two accounts are from *They Speak for Themselves*, compiled just after the War on Poverty was announced and the Civil Rights Act passed but before they were implemented:

"You Gotta Have a Good Neighbor or Mama"

Sure, some people on welfare are resentful. I'd say those most resentful are those that held responsible jobs before, the ones where there was once a good working man in the family and the job moved out of the city or he lost his job.

When you get on welfare, they say you're lazy. They talk about people on welfare pretty bad.

You go down to the welfare office on Washington Boulevard and you take a physical. If you pass the physical, they put you to work.

If a holiday comes up, maybe we are thrown two days behind in getting our check.

On welfare now, you can eat good maybe two or three days a month. If you got little kids, you might be able to substitute little things so they won't notice so much. But with teenagers, they'll just go elsewhere.

Then you gotta have a good neighbor or Mama or a brother or some-body on the side.

But most people try to send their kids to school no matter how poor they are. And these kids are the future soldiers of war. They don't ask then if you had to drink powdered milk. They only want to know if you got two arms and two legs and even then they don't care.

They keep talking to us about feeding the kids oatmeal and peanut butter. I don't think their kids like oatmeal. I wonder what they'd do if they took a survey and found out people are feeding their kids cornflakes and pancakes for breakfast. That's what they get for one man trying to put 55,000 people on welfare on one diet.

Say, what do you think poor people's luxuries are? It's the smiles on one another's faces. That what it is.

"Sometimes a Little Vegetable Soup"

All I can say is I do the best. The ADC (the Aid to Dependent Children program) is practically all I got to live with. I don't know how other people are faring on it.

All of us need clothing. For meals, we have peas as greens, rice, salm-on, the kind you can get cheap in a can. And we have pork and beans, leg bones, and sometimes a little vegetable soup.

 I buy the cheapest I can. I buy clothes from the Goodwill. When you buy clothes from there, sometimes the minute you put them on they wear out. They have the dry rot and they're no good. But you got to keep something on your kids. I bought my son a pair of pants. I only washed them once and the knee is out and they are bust in the back. Sometimes though you can buy pretty good things there.

Most everything you put your hands on costs a lot of money. I have to pay a babysitter when I go to the doctor and I'm simply not able to pay the price for a good pair of shoes.

Will it get better or worse? I think everybody with a family has the same hope it will be better. I would like to see my children grow up to have it better than it is for me. I wouldn't like it to be like this for them.

I'm in good hopes that civil rights and this poverty thing will come through. It wouldn't help me, but my children it will help them. I may be gone, but I know it would be better for them.

* * *

Such a mother's hopes and selflessness, as expressed in the final para-graph of her comments, encapsulate the idea and hopes engendered by declaring war on poverty. Good things were achieved for the "millions," as President Johnson promised they would be as the War on Poverty succeeded.

The following four studies are among the most respected that discuss the effects on welfare as "income transfer" and poverty programs such as those that made up the War on Poverty. Each affords statistical analysis illustrating the positive effects of the War on Poverty to reduce poverty:

1. Lane Kenworthy, "Do social-welfare policies reduce poverty? A cross-national assessment," *Social Forces* 77, no 3 (1999), 1119–1139;

2. David Bradley, Evelyne Huber, Stephanie Moller, François Nielson, John D. Stephens, "Determinants of relative poverty in advanced capitalist democracies," *American Sociological Review*, 68, no. 1 (Feb. 2003), 22–51;

3. David Brady, "The Welfare State and Relative Poverty in Rich Western Democracies," Luxembourg Income Study Working Paper Series Paper No. 390 (Oct. 2004), 1967–1997;

4. Isabel V. Sawhill, a senior fellow at Brookings Institute, did an analysis of "Poverty in the United States" that is also available online in *The Concise Encyclopedia of Economics.*

Even Rebecca M. Blank, a persuasive critic of liberal economics acknowledged, "Many of our antipoverty efforts have accomplished exactly what they set out to accomplish" (cf. Luxenburg study listed above).

Michael B. Katz, the author of *The Undeserving Poor: From the War on Poverty to the War on Welfare* (Pantheon Books, 1989) goes right at the assumptions and assertion that critics have used in judging the War on Poverty. He wrote:

> Between 1964 and 1972, the federal government unleashed a barrage of new antipoverty programs. Those most directly associated with the Office of Economic Opportunity fought poverty by trying to expand opportunity and empower local communities. Others radically altered the procedures that redistributed income. ...
>
> Public memory, and much subsequent history, treats the War on Poverty harshly. The nation fought a war on poverty and poverty won, has become a summary judgment assented to without reservation even by many liberals. These years deserve a more discriminating verdict.
>
> Although the Great Society did not alter the structure of social welfare, its accomplishments belie contemporary conventional wisdom that either ignores or belittles the great achievements of the

era. Although social policy did not seriously dent the forces that generate want, although many new programs failed spectacularly and others disappointed their sponsors, the federal government did alleviate the consequences of poverty. ...

Between 1965 and 1972, the government transfer programs lifted about half the poor over the poverty line. Between 1959 and 1980, the proportion of elderly poor people dropped, almost entirely as a result of government transfer programs from 35 percent to 16 percent. Medicare and Medicaid improved health care dramatically. In 1963, one of every five Americans who lived below the poverty line never had been examined by a physician, and poor people used medical facilities far less than others. By 1970, the proportion never examined had dipped to 8 percent, and the proportion visiting a physician annually was about the same as for everyone else. Between 1965 and 1972, poor women began to consult physicians far more often during pregnancy, and infant mortality dropped 33 percent. Food stamps successfully reduced hunger, and housing programs lessened overcrowding and the number of people living in substandard housing.

Of course, there are less sanguine ways to read the evidence: poverty remained unacceptably high; millions of Americans still lacked medical insurance; in the 1980s, housing became a major problem for just about everyone with a low income, and hunger reappeared as a national disgrace. Indeed, as the rate of poverty before transfer programs shows, neither public policy nor private enterprise had moderated the great forces that generate poverty in America. At best, they alleviate its effects. Nevertheless, the expansion of social welfare benefits from 1964 to 1972 transformed the lives of millions of Americans and demonstrated the capacity of government as an agent of social change.

In 1986, the American Catholic Bishops issued a document, *Economic Justice for All: A Pastoral Letter on Catholic Social Teaching and the U.S. Economy.* In its pages (which are available online), they assessed the results of the War on Poverty, writing that:

> Although the task of alleviating poverty is complex and demanding, we should be encouraged by examples of our nation's past successes in this area. Our history shows that we can reduce poverty. During the 1960s and early 1970s, the official poverty rate was cut in half, due not only to a healthy economy, but also to

public policy decisions that improved the nation's income transfer programs. It is estimated, for example, that in the late 1970s federal benefit programs were lifting out of poverty about 70 percent of those who would have otherwise been poor.

During the last twenty-five years, the Social Security Program has dramatically reduced poverty among the elderly. In addition, in 1983 it lifted out of poverty almost 1.5 million children of re-tired, deceased and disabled workers. Medicare has enhanced the life expectancy and health status of elderly and disabled people, and Medicaid has reduced infant mortality and greatly improved access to health care for the poor. These and other successful so-cial welfare programs are evidence of our nation's commitment to social justice and a decent life for everyone. They also indicate that we have the capacity to design programs that are effective and provide necessary assistance to the needy in a way that respects their dignity.

Section 6

PEOPLE AND ORGANIZATIONS TAKING ACTION TO END POVERTY

We stand on the threshold of a unique awakening to poverty's brutality, unfairness, and pervasiveness.

39

Half in Ten and Its Reality Check

BY MELISSA BOTEACH

The first chapter of this book begins with the question, "Are you poor?" The author mentions a conversation with a woman sitting waiting for public transportation. She answered that query by stating that a reality check tells her that she and her family are poor because they are forced to rely on government help even to get by.

In representing Half in Ten, we too face a reality check. As our name indicates, our goal is to cut the poverty in this country by half within ten years.

"Can they do it?" you have every right to ask.

The answer is, "Not by ourselves."

But we never set off to do it alone. By working with others, we can cut poverty in half.

You are one of those others.

About Half in Ten

Half in Ten's mission is to build the political and public will to cut U.S. poverty in half in ten years. Our goal is not simply to move families one dollar above the poverty line, but to build a grassroots movement to enact policies that create good jobs, strengthen families, and promote economic security so that we grow the middle-class.

Given stagnant wages, the concentration of wealth, and high rates of hunger in the past decade, it's easy to dismiss such a target as a "pie in the sky" goal. But this dejection is misplaced. Throughout our history, we *have* cut poverty in half. From 1949 to 1959, the poverty rate fell by nearly half—from 40.5 percent to 22.4 percent—and from 1959 to 1973, we cut in half again all the way down to 11.1 percent. When we have shared economic growth coupled with public and private initiatives to grow the middle-class, we can make huge strides in increasing opportunity and economic security for all Americans.

So, What's the Plan? How Do We Get There?

In 2007, Half in Ten partner, Center for American Progress, released a report emphasized three policies:

- increasing the minimum wage to its historic level of half the average wage,
- making the tax code work better for working families by expanding the earned income tax credit and child tax credit,
- and making childcare fully available as a work support for low-income families.

These three changes in course would cut poverty by 26 percent, getting us more than halfway to the target. Our recent report, "Restoring Shared Prosperity" starts the clock on our goal to cut poverty in half. It offers updated policy solutions to create good jobs, strengthen families, and ensure economic security.

Our job is then to educate and mobilize people across the country to fight for these policies and hold our elected officials accountable for progress. In practice, this means we work in coalition with dozens of other organizations and engage thousands of grassroots activists across the country to win policy victories that move families from poverty to prosperity.

Half in Ten in Action

For example, in the fall of 2010, expansions in the earned income tax credit (EITC) and child tax credit, policies that boost the incomes of low-wage workers, were set to expire. If Congress failed to act, millions of working families would have been pushed into poverty and 18 million low-income kids would have been affected.

As the expiration of the tax credits loomed, Half in Ten pulled together a public event on the importance of the tax credits, and a large-scale webinar of over 1,000 participants featuring elected officials, advocates, and low-income workers who stood to lose their tax credits if Congress failed to act. We used the event and webinar to make the stakes clear and provide new resources to activists across the country including: fact sheets, sample letters to Congress, and social media actions, mobilizing thousands to take action throughout the fall. In the end, the EITC and child tax credit improvements were included in the December 2010 tax deal.

We believe that in mobilizing to win policy victories, the voices of low-income families speaking on their own behalf are critical. For example, Barbie, a working mom made a compelling case for tax credits for working families at a Half in Ten event:

I'm a mother of two children and I work full-time. I am sitting here, as a witness to be able to tell you that the earned income tax credit changed my life … It made me independent. Working was something I've always done, always wanted to do, but I struggled making ends meet because I raised my two children on my own. Because of it I was able to stabilize myself in my own home, where I don't have to worry about bugs walking down the wall … where I don't have to worry about my children asking me, "Mom, why can't I take a shower?" and I have to tell them, "We don't have any hot water today."

I was a victim of domestic abuse for seven years, and the earned income tax credit constantly provided me the security to be able to say, "This year I'm gonna get out" and I would, and he would find me, and I'd go through it all over again. But just because of the amount I received through it last year, I haven't had to turn back to that situation. I'm blessed to be able to provide a life for my children, which they've never seen before."

We Need You

We know we can do it. We have a plan. What we need is political and it is creating the public will.

There are a number of ways that you can get involved in helping achieve the goal of cutting poverty in half over the next decade. In addition to volunteering in your local community and getting involved in direct service, here are a few ways you can help push our elected officials to enact policies to cut poverty in half:

Sign the Pledge
http://halfinten.org/pledge/individual/

Taking this step will make sure that you get a monthly alert with all the resources to call or use to write your members of Congress on timely issues that affect low-income families. We have helped mobilized thousands of people to call their elected officials on policies to create jobs, strengthen the safety net, and protect low-income families against damaging budget cuts. The more people that call or write their elected representatives, the more they feel the pressure to stand up and champion policies to help cut poverty in half!

Tell Us Your Story!

Andy Goodman once said, "No one ever marched on Washington because of a pie chart." While good data is critical, our personal stories are also a powerful vehicle to move people into action and force elected officials to come face to face with the human consequences of their policy decisions. Go to www.halfinten.org/stories/submit and tell us how programs on the chopping block, such as childcare subsidies, nutrition assistance, or the earned income tax credit have helped you achieve the American Dream. Tell us what cuts to the safety net would mean to you, your family, and your community. Half in Ten posts the stories at **www.halfinten.org/stories** and works to connect storytellers to advocacy and media opportunities so that they can speak in their own voice about steps we need to take to ensure shared prosperity for all.

Download Our Action Toolkit at
http://halfinten.org/indicators/publications/toolkit

We designed this toolkit to help readers like you take their interest in poverty and move it into action in their communities. It provides background information and data on poverty and policy solutions, as well as tips on starting an advocacy campaign, organizing your community, conducting media outreach, and building relationships with your elected officials. It can take your advocacy to the next level and bring a Half in Ten campaign to your community. We stand ready to help.

Conclusion

The first chapter of this book begins with the question, "Are you poor?" But the reality is all of us are impoverished by the existence of poverty in our communities. Poverty diminishes America's competitiveness by limiting the potential of our workers, reducing consumer buying power, diminishing educational outcomes, and increasing healthcare costs.

A goal to cut poverty in half is one

- to bring 23 million more people into the middle class;
- to send more kids to school well fed and ready to learn;
- to prepare more workers to participate in building the jobs and industries of tomorrow; and
- to include more Americans in the economy so that our country is more competitive and provides greater opportunity for all its citizens.

It's a down payment on a goal to end poverty once and for all in the richest country the world has ever known.

We can achieve these goals. By working with others, we *can* cut poverty in half. You are one of those others.

40

FRAC: Eradicating Hunger and Undernutrition

For meals we have mostly neck bones, white potatoes, spaghetti, beans
and things like that. We try all the stores to get bargains.
We keep going. We do what we can do.
—A FATHER OF TEN IN 1965, WORKING AS A JANITOR
(BEFORE THE SNAP FOOD STAMP PROGRAM)

FRAC (Food Research and Action Center, http://frac.org) is a leading national nonprofit organization working to improve public policies and public-private partnerships to eradicate hunger and undernutrition in the United States. To accomplish this—to address hunger, food insecurity, and their root cause, poverty—we work with hundreds of national, state and local nonprofit organizations, public agencies, corporations, and labor organizations

The following two FRAC press releases dramatically show ways in which it works to inform America about hunger and undernutrition issues:

FRAC Releases New Polling Data Showing Overwhelming Support for Efforts to End Hunger
Washington, D.C. – January 19, 2012
By an overwhelming margin, American voters oppose cutting food stamp assistance (the Supplemental Nutrition Assistance Program, or SNAP) as a way to reduce government spending, according to new poll data released today by the Food Research and Action Center (FRAC). Seventy-seven percent of voters say this is the wrong way to reduce spending and only 15 percent favor cutting such assistance.

- The opposition to cutting food stamps crossed party lines: 92 percent of Democrats, 74 percent of Independents, and 63 percent of Republicans say this is the wrong way to reduce spending.

- Only nine percent of those polled said they would be more likely to support a candidate who favors cutting funds for the food stamp program; half said they would be less likely.

- Opposition to food stamp cuts is even more overwhelming than in polling data FRAC released in November 2010, when 71 percent said it was the wrong way to cut spending.

Voters are broadly concerned about the nation's hunger problem: 81 percent say that low-income families and children not being able to afford enough food to eat is a serious problem.

The poll of 1,013 registered voters was conducted by Hart Research Associates from January 11–17, 2012. Support for ending hunger and protecting food stamps was high across party lines, age, race, gender, income, and geographical areas.

Food stamp benefits currently go to one in seven Americans, a historically high participation rate that is largely attributable to a poor economy and the added millions of working families struggling with hunger. FRAC commissioned this poll to measure support for anti-hunger measures generally and for food stamps in particular, at a time when Congress is returning for a new session, and when some state policymakers (e.g., in Michigan and Pennsylvania), some conservatives in Congress, and some political leaders have launched attacks on the program. The poll shows that a majority of Americans believe that that the Food Stamp Program is very important to the country, and strongly believe that the federal government should have a major role in the effort to provide low-income people with the food and nutrition they need.

"What this poll tells us is that, despite rhetoric and false claims about the program, Americans across the country see food stamps as a program that works and that is making a real difference for people," said FRAC President Jim Weill. "We urge all national and state policymakers to recognize SNAP's strengths as an essential support for Americans. With high rates of hunger, poverty, and unemployment, SNAP is helping millions of families put food on the table. American voters won't tolerate hunger in our midst, and across party lines they support this valuable program.

FRAC Report Outlines Strategies Needed to Support Households' Ability to Afford Fresh Fruits and Vegetables
Washington, D.C. – December 15, 2011

A new report (by the Food Research and Action Center (FRAC) provides a unique look at the struggle to access healthy food that is being faced by millions of Americans, and especially low-income people.

Among all households across the years 2008-2010, 8.2 percent of respondents reported that it was "not easy to get affordable fresh fruits and vegetables." But those with household incomes less than $24,000/year reported such affordability and access challenges 2.5 times more frequently (13.8 percent) than those with incomes between $60,000 and $89,999 (5.7 percent).

The report analyzes how the struggle by households to obtain affordable healthy food presents itself by race, income, health status, and in different parts of the country. Containing data down to the congressional district, FRAC's report analyzes the answers given by hundreds of thousands of survey respondents to a question posed for the Gallup-Healthways Well-Being Index project: "In the city or area where you live, is it easy or not easy to get affordable fresh fruits and vegetables." FRAC characterizes "not easy" answers as evidence of an affordability and access challenge.

Among the biggest differences observed were those between income groups, and for those who experienced food hardship (an inability to afford enough food based on another Gallup question). Among those in households with food hardship, 18.5 percent reported affordability and accessibility problems, while only 5.7 percent of those in households without food hardship reported such challenges.

Other findings include:

- Hispanics and Blacks reported considerably higher rates of difficulty in accessing affordable fresh fruits and vegetables, compared to Whites and Asians.

- Among people reporting poor health status, the prevalence of fruit and vegetable affordability and access challenges was four times that of people reporting excellent health status (20.0 percent vs. 5.0 percent).

"A household's ability to access healthy food hinges on having enough resources to do so. What the data in our analysis show is that access and affordability are household economic insecurity problems as well as community 'food desert' problems," said Jim Weill, FRAC President. "The remedies have to centrally include supporting families' ability to purchase healthier food."

Among remedies the report proposes are: efforts at the federal level to increase the adequacy of SNAP (food stamps) benefits so they go further; rejection of recent proposals in Congress to reduce SNAP benefits; increased outreach and reduced red tape at the state level so more people receive SNAP; assuring that stores accept SNAP EBT cards and WIC vouchers; and stronger efforts at the community level to increase the number of outlets offering healthy food.

41

Just Harvest—Pittsburgh, PA

BY TARA MARKS

Just Harvest is a membership organization that works in the Pittsburgh area toward the elimination of hunger and poverty.

While I now have a master's degree in business administration and have served as its executive director, I also know what it means to go hungry, so hungry that you nearly faint from it and cannot keep your bearings.

It is why I especially care and do the work I do.

First as a volunteer and then in a full time capacity, I have been able to make the effort so that it won't happen to others as it did to me. Hunger and poverty, I want to see end.

It got to the point where, one weekend my son and I had had enough eggs, milk and bread if I rationed them out for the next three days, but there would be only enough for my son. I had none for myself. I did not eat Friday, Saturday and Sunday.

On Monday morning when I attempted to drive to the job I did have, I had to pullover to the side of the road. I was confused and nearly passed out from hunger.

I learned what hunger meant. It hurts and you get to the point where the body stops asking for food.

I got there in the same way any number of other women have. When our son was born we agreed that I would be a normal stay-at-home mom. But later, my son's father left us and took everything with him.

I had to move into a public housing project, where selling drugs and violence were common. I applied for food stamps, but that was a disaster. I waited three and a half hours to meet with a social worker. He warned me they would investigate me and I could go to jail if they decided anything I said was fraudulent. He had me thoroughly scared. I gave up and walked out.

Sometime after that I was at a parenting meeting at a day care center for single parent families. Representatives of Just Harvest were there and spoke about getting food stamps.

They listened to me, sent me back to the food stamp office to try again, told me how to apply and even gave me a booklet on it.

They believed in me even when I did not believe in myself. I did go back and started receiving food stamps. What a difference they made!

Some of the mothers in the projects where I was living are the smartest women I ever met, especially when it comes to stretching a dollar and raising their kids. I learned a lot from them. Still, poverty can be overwhelming. The poor often, I realized, need someone who can help in situations such as I had found myself in.

From then on, I was determined to do anything I could to help other women so they would never have to go through what I had. For two years, I volunteered with Just Harvest, which does exactly that. In the Pittsburgh area alone, it has helped some 5,000 people file applications for food stamps. We are also advocates for adequate funding for nutritional programs for the poor and provide welfare advocates for anyone with problems in dealing with aid agencies.

Eventually, I was able to get my college degree and then a master's. I also met a wonderful man, remarried, and we now have a blended family with four children.

I was looking for a job and saw an ad for Co-director of Just Harvest. I could not believe my good fortune. I applied and got the position.

Just Harvest has developed a Food Stamp Program Assistant program that helps around 100 people each month apply for SNAP/food stamps and overcome barriers that keep them from accessing these very important benefits.

We also have a free service that helps poor people file for their earned income tax credits, which many do not know about.

One of the major things we seek to do is increase participation in the programs that provide nutritional assistance to poor families. We have nine staff members as well as several interns. The staff includes two staff food stamp experts and a welfare advocate.

There is an advantage in coming from among those who have suffered real hunger. I have told my story and testified in behalf of Just Harvest and the people it serves before both the state legislature and the U.S. Congress. I have talked of my experience and pleaded with them to help.

Our goal is to make certain that people are able to have food on their tables. I have moved out of the projects but still have strong feelings for those whom I left behind there.

42

A Minnesota Without Poverty—Saint Paul, MN

The following is based on an interview with Nancy Maeker, the executive director of A Minnesota Without Poverty:

A Minnesota Without Poverty began in 2001 in the Saint Paul Area when a religious group debated whether eliminating poverty in Saint Paul should be through advocacy or charity. The group has now become an effective statewide movement determined to end poverty in Minnesota by 2020.

The program first evolved from a discussion group into an ecumenical and interfaith initiative to end poverty. Now it is a 501(c)(3) nonprofit and, as such, seeks to engage all sectors of society—faith communities, government, business, people experiencing poverty, communities of color, nonprofits, and foundations.

In 2004, religious leaders from across the state signed A Common Foundation: Shared Principles for Work on Overcoming Poverty.

In 2006, A Minnesota Without Poverty sponsored a Focus on Poverty event, in partnership with the Archdiocese of Minneapolis and Saint Paul. Then-Senator John Hottinger attended that event, saw the "Common Foundation" for the first time and heard the question: What do we need to do to end poverty in Minnesota by 2020? He went back to the capitol and wrote the bill to create the Legislative Commission to End Poverty in Minnesota by 2020. He used the text of the Common Foundation in the bill.

It passed with support from both parties. In 2007 and 2008, the bipartisan Legislative Commission to End Poverty in Minnesota by 2020 held twelve listening sessions throughout the state, and its members made recommendations for eliminating poverty in Minnesota.

In January 2009, A Minnesota Without Poverty sponsored a public launching of the recommendations at Landmark Center, St. Paul. The theme of that event was "If Not We, Then Who? If Not Now, Then When?"

Its Recommendations to End Poverty in Minnesota by 2020 included:

- Restore work as a way out of poverty.
- Ensure that work pays
- Make work available
- Help business make employment opportunities available
- Refocus public assistance to streamline services and support everyone's capacity and potential.

A Minnesota Without Poverty also helped to pass the Ladder Out of Poverty bill, as well as joined forces with the Half In Ten Campaign—a national effort to cut poverty in half in ten years.

Volunteers do much work for A Minnesota Without Povery. They include the board, a Statewide Organizing Team, and five active workgroups.

The Arts and Media Workgroup uses the arts and media as vehicles to build an awareness that can lead to action and results in ending poverty. Its members originated the theme of "Enough for All," and used it in depicting artists' interpretations of "enough."

The Business Catalyst Workgroup facilitates entrepreneurial opportunities in rural and immigrant communities, and communities of color—with full participation of people in poverty in these communities. They have created the Micro-Enterprise Catalyst Partnership, which partners with local congregations or nonprofits to initiate a micro-loan process in various communities in the state. One of those partnerships is The Art Shoppe at Midtown Global Market, in Minneapolis, which supports ten artists/entrepreneurs. One among the ten artists is a woman who was homeless and draws very imaginative and well-done images of ordinary life on paper bags.

The Development Workgroup recently sponsored its first annual fundraising dinner to generate financial support for the work of ending poverty in Minnesota.

The Public Policy workgroup identifies the annual legislative agenda and initiates appropriate public action to promote this agenda. This workgroup has planned and produced the three videos starring the Minnesota Church Ladies—brief videos, available on YouTube, which use humor to address serious public policy issues. They are also leading the implementation of the Legislative Commission to End Poverty recommendations.

The Education Workgroup creates and promotes educational materials and resources for engaging all sectors of society in the work of ending poverty. They have produced a six-session, interfaith resource, "Enough for All: A Discussion Guide for People of Faith."

The movement is open to everyone—regardless of age, race, ethnicity, citizenship, religion, sexual orientation, or gender—and invites all to participate in ending poverty throughout Minnesota by 2020.

We believe there is enough for all to have enough, if we all do our part.

Our website is *http://www.facebook.com/pages/A-Minnesota-Without-Poverty/*.

43

The Annie E. Casey Foundation

BY MICHAEL LARACY

Since 1948, the Annie E. Casey Foundation has worked to build better futures for disadvantaged children and their families in the United States.

Annie E. Casey Foundation is a private charitable organization, dedicated to helping build better futures for disadvantaged children in the United States. It was established in 1948 by Jim Casey, one of the founders of UPS, and his siblings, who named the Foundation in honor of their mother.

Casey, who initially served as chief executive officer of UPS, once said that "what is needed is a renewed determination to think creatively, to learn from what has succeeded and what has failed, and, perhaps most important, to foster a sense of common commitment among all those concerned with the welfare of children."

Over the years, the Annie E. Casey Foundation has tried to grow its agenda, ambition, and vision in ways consistent with its founding.

The primary mission of the Foundation is to foster public policies, human-service reforms, and community supports that more effectively meet the needs of today's vulnerable children and families. In pursuit of this goal, the Foundation makes grants that help states, cities and neighborhoods fashion more innovative, cost-effective responses to these needs.

Since 1948, the Annie E. Casey Foundation has worked to build better futures for disadvantaged children and their families in the United States. The primary mission of the Foundation is to foster public policies, human service reforms, and community supports that more meet the needs of today's vulnerable children and families.

I have been with the foundation for the last 18 years serving as its director of policy reform and advocacy. We distribute $15 million in grants to nonprofit organizations that are advocates in behalf of low-income families.

My interest began when I was in high school. I volunteered at Belle-vue Hospital, New York City's hospital that serves the very poor. I did so because I wanted to be a doctor; but, while I was there, I saw a greater need for work to be done in social policy and urban planning. I have been following through on that ever since.

One of our efforts is the Casey Foundation-supported KIDS COUNT, a national and state-by-state effort to track the status of children in the United States. By providing policymakers and citizens with benchmarks of child well being, it seeks to enrich local, state, and national discussions concerning ways to secure better futures for all children.

Another program we support is Spotlight on Poverty and Opportu-nity: The Source for News, Ideas and Action. It is a non-partisan initia-tive that brings together diverse perspectives from the political, policy, advocacy, and foundation communities to find genuine solutions to the economic hardship confronting millions of Americans. Through the on-going exchange of ideas, research, and data, Spotlight seeks to inform the policy debate about reducing poverty and increasing opportunity in the United States.

In general, our grant making is limited to initiatives in the United States that have significant potential to demonstrate innovative policy, service delivery, and community supports for disadvantaged children and families. Most grantees have been invited by the Foundation to par-ticipate in these projects. For example, we help support Half in Ten, which brings together organizations fighting to cut poverty in the United States.

One of the efforts with which we were involved that has made a dif-ference has been our support for organizations that advocated for stimu-lus money to help the very poor through an increase in the food stamp program and initiation of the earned income tax credit for the working poor.

Jim Casey once said that "what is needed is a renewed determination to think creatively, to learn from what has succeeded and what has failed, and, perhaps most important, to foster a sense of common commitment among all those concerned with the welfare of children."

We have tried to live up to that.

44

Witnesses to Hunger—Philadelphia, PA

BY MARIANA CHILTON, DIRECTOR

Several times, I have given testimony before Congress as an expert witness on hunger and poverty. I am not the expert witness, however. Rather, the women whom I have interviewed, who are caught in poverty and who have suffered real hunger are.

Barbara, for example, talks about being so hungry after she had not eaten for days, she has found herself staring at the pizza ads that were dropped off at her door in hopes that looking at them would give her the feel of having eaten something. She had given up everything she had so her child had something to eat.

Very often when a person is enduring hunger you find that she had the same experience as a child.

Latetia told me that her own mother was an alcoholic and put next to no effort into feeding her children. As a result, they attempted to make food of whatever they could find. In her case, it had been flour. They had mixed it with water and fried it. They found a package of breadcrumbs and put them into what they were frying.

Crystal tells about the experience of being on welfare and how much it helps to improvise. All three of her children are on Medicaid because they have major health problems and she is very concerned that she keep in good physical shape so she can continue to care for them. She wishes somehow she could afford to join a health club to be able to do that.

They are the experts, but they talk a different language than the people who provide the services that they so much need. If you talk about them having rights and about justice, they laugh at it. They have the experience of not ever being taken seriously, of never getting their rights and not experiencing justice. They see themselves as invisible.

What they can tell us about is the connection of hunger and poverty to violence. They daily experience violence from the people around them, their partners, people on drugs, the police, and a myriad of others. They believe poverty and violence are inseparable.

They often believe they are not in a position to be heard when they speak for themselves and tell the intimate experience of not having food or, when they have something to eat, it does afford the right nutrition. Consequently, we have worked out with low-income mothers ways to speak and to testify for themselves.

They have accompanied us when we gave staff briefings on the Hill or when we have testified. But we have wanted them to be able to do more. Photos they take are proving a unique way to do this and we have given them cameras to take pictures of the poverty they face day in and day out.

A number of them have done it and come up with incredible, powerful photographs. We have put these pictures on exhibit, including in the Capitol Rotunda gallery. Through them, the women have been able to tell their stories.

One example was Jean, a witness from Scranton, Pennsylvania, who took a photo of the small pile of change and added the comment, "That was all I had. So many things needed to be done with that change. It's just overbearing. It's hard to handle."

We call the whole project of gathering testimony from low-income individuals and using it to move people and change our nation, "Witness to Hunger."

Several other cities have shown interest in creating a similar project in their areas and we are putting together a how-to booklet to help them.

What we seek to do is engage those who have experienced poverty as full partners in developing research and policies that work and to engage in an on-going national dialogue on poverty.

The enormous amount of poverty, hunger and poor nutrition among the people of this country has to change and we need to involve those who have experienced them into the process. We need their words, their experiences and their photo images to do it.

Dr. Mariana Chilton, PhD MPH, an associate professor of public health at the Drexel University School of Public Heath in Philadelphia, has served as the principal investigator for the Philadelphia GROW Project—a nutrition and growth initiative for children and their families. She investigates the health impacts of hunger and food insecurity among young children zero to three. Her work spans across a variety of issues that affect low-income individuals. She recently launched Witnesses to Hunger to increase women's participation in the national dialogue on hunger and poverty.

$$\text{45}$$

CLASP and Spotlight on Poverty

CLASP (Center for Law and Social Policy) is a national antipoverty policy organization that has been on the American scene since 1969. Its stated mission is to improve the lives of low-income people.

CLASP has a clear and resonant voice in the halls of Congress and statehouses throughout the nation. It uses it "to develop and advocate for federal, state, and local policies to strengthen families and create pathways to education and work."

Among those praising its work has been Gwen Moore (D-WI), U.S. House of Representatives, who said: "Even if members don't agree, they can't run from what CLASP has to say. Their work is solid, thorough and extremely well-respected on the Hill."

In a similar vein, Deepak Bhargave, Executive Director, Center for Community Change, stated: "CLASP plays a unique role in advancing anti-poverty initiatives in this country that makes it a national treasure and an indispensable resource."

The vast extent of its efforts can be seen in projects such as producing and releasing a well-received video, *In Their Own Words,* which vividly describes the experiences of young men of color who had dropped out or were expelled from school, and how "disconnected-youth"-focused programs help put them on a path to education and work.

CLASP also manages an independent foundation/nonpartisan initiative—Spotlight on Poverty and Opportunity: The Source for News, Ideas and Action.

It seeks "to bring together diverse perspectives from the political, policy, advocacy and foundation communities to find genuine solutions to the economic hardship confronting millions of Americans. Through the ongoing exchange of ideas, research and data, Spotlight seeks to inform the policy debate about reducing poverty and increasing opportunity in the United States."

Spotlight on Poverty and Opportunity was launched in October 2007 by major U.S. foundations to foster nonpartisan debate during the 2008 campaign season about policy approaches for addressing poverty and opportunity. Today, Spotlight provides a platform for ongoing discussion about how best to address the needs of those who have fallen into poverty during the Great Recession and those who have struggled for generations to move up the economic ladder.

Spotlight is one of the leading nonpartisan forums on poverty in the country, known for presenting "big tent" ideas and solutions for reducing poverty and increasing economic opportunity through its comprehensive website, weekly e-newsletter, policy events, and original research and surveys. It has attracted interest from public figures of all political stripes to write for the website's commentary section, participate in webcasts, and rely on the one-stop shop website for the latest news, research, data, and commentary about poverty and opportunity.

The following is an index of campaigns to fight poverty and increase opportunity provided by Spotlight on Poverty and Opportunity. *The Book of the Poor*'s author has added several that are marked with asterisks.

Alliance to End Hunger (http://www.alliancetoendhunger.org/)

*A Minnesota Without Poverty (http://www.mnwithoutpoverty.org/)

Bread for the World (http://www.bread.org/)

Call to Renewal (http://www.calltorenewal.com/)

Campaign to End Childhood Hunger (http://www.frac.org/)

Catholic Charities USA Campaign to Reduce Poverty in America (http://www.catholiccharitiesusa.org/poverty/)

Catholic Campaign for Human Development (http://www.usccb.org/about/catholic-campaign-for-human-development/)

Center for Community Change Campaign for Community Values (http://www.communityactionpartnership.org/)

Coalition on Human Needs (http://www.infochn.org/)

Community Action Partnership: Rooting Out Poverty (http://www.communityactionpartnership.com/)

*Feed My Starving Children (http://www.fmsc.org/)

*Florida CHAIN (http://www.floridachain.org/)

Half in Ten (http://www.halfinten.org/)

Jewish Council For Public Affairs: Confronting Poverty (http://www.jewishpublicaffairs.org/)

*Just Harvest (http://www.justharvest.org/)

Let Justice Roll (http://www.letjusticeroll.org/index.html/)

Make Poverty History (http://www.one.org/)

Marguerite Casey Foundation's Equal Voice for America's Families Campaign (http://www.equalvoiceforfamilies.org/)

*National Alliance to End Homelessness (www.endhomelessness.org)

National League of Cities Municipal Action to Reduce Poverty Project (http://www.nlc.org/)

National Symposium on Poverty and Economic Security (http://www.cencomfut.com/ncpes.htm/)

Opportunity Nation (http://www.opportunitynation.org/)

*Sojourners (tking@sojo.net)

*Spotlight on Poverty and Opportunity (http://www.spotlightonpoverty.org/)

*Tennessee Health Care Campaign (www.thcc2.org)

The National Urban Alliance for Effective Education (http://www.nuatc.org/)

The New England Consortium (http://www.endpovertynewengland.org/)

The One Campaign (http://www.one.org/)

U.S. Conference of Mayors Poverty Work and Opportunity Task Force (http://www.mayors.org/USCM/uscm_projects_services/workingfamilies/taskforce.asp/)

*Witnesses to Hunger (http://www.witnessestohunger.org/)

Working Poor Families Project (http://www.workingfamilies.org/)

46

PolicyLink: Equity in Tomorrow's America

BY SARAH TREUHAFT, ANGELA GLOVER BLACKWELL,

AND MANUEL PASTOR

PolicyLink is a national research and action institute advancing economic and social equity by Lifting Up What Works®. The following article appeared in Race, Poverty & the Environment, *vol. 18, no. 2, 2011:*

As the country witnesses the emergence of a new racial and ethnic majority, equity—long a matter of social justice and morality—is now also an economic imperative. The nation can only achieve and sustain growth and prosperity by integrating all into the economy, including those who have too often been left behind. America's Tomorrow describes the components of an equity-driven growth model and acknowledges that a true social movement is needed to achieve equity.

America Needs a New Growth Model

The nation's current economic model is broken. The problem is not just the recent economic downturn, as pressing and important as that has been. Over the past several decades, economic growth has slowed, racial and income inequality has spiked, and the middle class has withered.

America needs a new strategy to bring about robust growth that is widely shared by all who live within its borders. The new growth model must embrace the nation's changing demographics, and make the investments needed to allow the next generation to reach its full potential.

The United States is undergoing a major demographic transformation in which the racial and ethnic groups that have been most excluded are now becoming a larger portion of the population. By 2042, the majority of the population will be people of color. Because youth are at the forefront of the nation's demographic transition, there is a growing racial generation gap between America's oldest and youngest: Eighty percent of seniors are white, compared with 54 percent of those under age 18.

Too many elders and decision makers do not see themselves reflected in the faces of the next generation, and they are not investing in the same educational systems and community infrastructure that enabled their own success.

This racial generation gap does not only put youth of color at risk, but it threatens the well being of all children and the nation as a whole.

Racial and Economic Inclusion
Will Help America Grow and Compete

Reducing inequality, growing the middle class, and turning today's youth and workers into tomorrow's skilled workers and innovators are critical to restoring America's growth and competitiveness. Given the nation's demographic transition, its leaders must address the wide racial disparities in educational outcomes, income, health, wealth, and employment that drag down the economy and hold back its potential.

Reducing Inequality Is Good for Growth

Increasingly, economists are finding that inequality is not only bad for those at the bottom of the income spectrum, but places everyone's economic future at risk. Recent studies suggest that inequality hinders growth and that greater economic inclusion corresponds with more robust economic growth.

Diversity Is an Economic Asset

America's transformation into a world nation inside its borders can help it connect to—and succeed in—the global economy. Diverse perspectives help teams solve problems and can foster the innovation needed to grow the economy. Diverse communities also create new markets: by developing new enterprises and providing a significant consumer base for existing businesses.

Building a Skilled Workforce Is Critical to Securing
Our Economic Future

The jobs of tomorrow will require ever-higher levels of skills and education, but the nation's educational and workforce systems are not adequately preparing people for these jobs. Forty-five percent of all jobs in 2018 are projected to require at least an associate's degree, but among today's workers only 27 percent of African Americans, 26 percent of U.S.-born Latinos, and 14 percent of Latino immigrants have achieved this level of education. Closing the wide and persistent racial gap in educational attainment is the key to building the strong workforce that is the backbone of the American economy.

Implementing an Equity-Driven Growth Model

An equity-driven growth model would grow new jobs and bolster long-term competitiveness while at the same time ensuring that all—especially low-income people and people of color—have the opportunity to benefit from and cocreate that growth. *America's Tomorrow* highlights promising strategies that link vulnerable populations to good jobs and career pathways while strengthening their local and regional economies within three key arenas:

1. Rebuilding Our Public Infrastructure

High-quality public infrastructure—roads, transit lines, schools, bridges, sidewalks, etc.—is an essential ingredient for fostering competitive regions, and public investment in infrastructure projects is one of the best strategies available to create jobs and get dollars flowing in the economy after a downturn. By choosing infrastructure projects that maximize job opportunities, targeting infrastructure jobs and projects to the people and communities most in need of jobs, and creating opportunities for local and minority-owned businesses, communities can achieve equity and growth at the same time.

> **Example:** In St. Louis, Metropolitan Congregations United and the Transportation Equity Network got the Missouri Department of Transportation to agree to devote 30 percent of the workforce hours on a $500 million highway project to low-income apprentices, and 1/2 of 1 percent of the project budget to job training. Other cities and states have adopted similar workforce provisions, and advocacy groups are now working to incorporate a similar construction careers policy in the next multibillion-dollar federal transportation bill.

2. Growing New Businesses and New Jobs

Small businesses create two out of every three jobs in this country and are critical for providing economic opportunities for low-income communities and communities of color. Providing training support and linking entrepreneurs to larger-scale opportunities, larger markets, larger sources of capital, and larger economic development and growth strategies—can create more start-ups and help existing small businesses grow so that they generate more jobs for the people who need them most.

> **Example:** Since 1993, the Neighborhood Development Center in St. Paul has collaborated with community-based organizations

to help diverse residents start their own businesses. The center provides a 16-week entrepreneurship course and follows up with business start-up and expansion loans, ongoing business support and technical assistance, and low-cost commercial space through its seven business incubators. Five hundred graduates are currently operating businesses, sustaining 2,200 jobs in the community.

3. Preparing Workers for the Jobs of Tomorrow

The nation's public- and private-sector leaders need to create an education and workforce training system that equips current and future workers with the skills they need to thrive in the world of work. Ensuring that all workers—including those who face high barriers to employment—can get the advanced training or education needed to access "middle-skill" jobs that pay family-supporting wages and offer career growth is critical. For the low-income children who face the greatest risk of not succeeding in school or work, this preparation must begin before they enter kindergarten and last throughout their careers.

> **Example:** The Chambers of Commerce in Santa Ana and Los Angeles launched partnerships with their local school districts to bridge the growing gap between the education levels of their diverse youth populations and the needs of their employers. The Santa Ana Chamber created a jointly administered high school that trains students for careers in six growth industries (automotive and transportation, engineering and construction, global business, health care, manufacturing, and new media), while the Los Angeles Chamber has arranged summer jobs and internships for the students with thousands of employer partners.

It Takes a Movement

Only a real social movement can bring about the social, cultural, market, and political shifts needed to create an equitable and inclusive economy. Major shifts in policy and politics are needed at every level—from local job creation to national economic policy—and bringing about those shifts will require sustained advocacy and diverse leadership that spans generations, sectors, and issues. New champions for equity-driven growth, including unlikely ones, will need to emerge.

A new national conversation must begin about equity driven growth. This should be a broad and open discussion. Honest debates about how to move ahead will be critical; no one group has all the problems and no one leader has all the solutions. But what is clear is that the task of creating jobs and opportunities—for everyone—requires the nation's full attention.

For "growth" and "equity" to come together, all will need to stretch outside of their comfort zones. Growth advocates will need to stop seeing equity as something that hopefully trickles down from their efforts to attract and grow businesses, and recognize that racial and economic inclusion will help them achieve their primary goals of growth and competitiveness.

Equity advocates, who have traditionally focused on how the benefits of growth are divvied up, will need to concentrate more on generating job growth, and choose strategies that work with market forces to reach their equity goals. As the country nears its status as a people-of color majority nation, we must act—*now*—to prepare for the future. Equity is the superior growth model. It is the path to prosperity—for all.

47

Ending World Poverty:
Achievements and Shortfalls
Highlights from the 2011 Millennium Development Goals Report
BY SHA ZUKANG, UNDER-SECRETARY-GENERAL

FOR ECONOMIC AND SOCIAL AFFAIRS

This report is based on a master set of data that has been compiled by an Inter Agency and expert group led by the Department of Economic and Social Affairs of the United Nations Secretariat, in response to the wishes of the General Assembly. For details and a full copy of the report, go to http:// www.un.org/millenniumgoals/reports.shtml/.

Lives have been saved or changed for the better

More than 10 years have passed since world leaders established goals and targets to free humanity from extreme poverty, hunger, illiteracy, and disease. The Millennium Declaration and the MDG framework for accountability derived from it have inspired development efforts and helped set global and national priorities and focus subsequent actions. While more work lies ahead, the world has cause to celebrate, in part due to the continued economic growth of some developing countries and targeted interventions in critical areas. Increased funding from many sources has translated into the expansion of programs to deliver services and resources to those most in need. Here are some of the highlights:

- Poverty continues to decline in many countries and regions. Despite significant setbacks after the 2008–2009 economic downturn, exacerbated by the food and energy crisis, the world is still on track to reach the poverty-reduction target. By 2015, it is now expected that the global poverty rate will fall below 15 per cent, well under the 23 per cent target. This global trend, however, mainly reflects rapid growth in Eastern Asia, especially China.

- In education, some of the poorest countries have made the greatest strides. Burundi, Madagascar, Rwanda, Samoa, Sao Tome and Principe, Togo, and the United Republic of Tanzania have achieved or are nearing the goal of universal primary education. Considerable progress has also been made in Benin, Bhutan, Burkina Faso, Ethiopia, Guinea, Mali, Mozambique, and Niger, where net enrollment ratios in primary school increased by more than 25 percentage points from 1999 to 2009. With an 18-percentage point gain between 1999 and 2009, sub-Saharan Africa is the region with the best record of improvement.

- Targeted interventions have succeeded in reducing child mortality.

The number of deaths of children under the age of five declined from 12.4 million in 1990 to 8.1 million in 2009. This means that nearly 12,000 fewer children are dying each day. Between 2000 and 2008, the combination of improved immunization coverage and the opportunity for second-dose immunizations led to a 78 percent drop in measles deaths worldwide. These averted deaths represent one quarter of the decline in mortality from all causes among children under five.

- Increased funding and control efforts have cut deaths from malaria.

Through the hard work of governments, international partners, community health workers and civil society, deaths from malaria have been reduced by 20 percent worldwide—from nearly 985,000 in 2000 to 781,000 in 2009. This reduction was accomplished through critical interventions, including the distribution of insecticide-treated mosquito nets, which, in sub-Saharan Africa alone, are sufficient to cover 76 per cent of the population at risk. The largest absolute drops in malaria deaths were in Africa, where 11 countries have reduced malaria cases and deaths by over 50 percent.

- Investments in preventing and treating HIV are yielding results.

New HIV infections are declining steadily, led by sub-Saharan Africa. In 2009, an estimated 2.6 million people were newly infected with HIV—a drop of 21 per cent since 1997, when new infections peaked. Thanks to increased funding and the expansion of major programs, the number of people receiving antiretroviral therapy for HIV or AIDS increased 13-fold from 2004 to 2009. By end-2009, 5.25 million people were receiving such treatment in low- and middle-income countries—an increase of over 1.2 million people since December 2008. As a result, the number of AIDS-related deaths declined by 19 per cent over the same period.

- Effective strategies against tuberculosis are saving millions of lives.

Between 1995 and 2009, a total of 41 million tuberculosis patients were successfully treated, and up to 6 million lives were saved, because of effective international protocols for the treatment of tuberculosis. Worldwide, deaths attributed to the disease have fallen by more than one third since 1990.

- Every region has made progress in improving access to clean drinking water.

An estimated 1.1 billion people in urban areas and 723 million people in rural areas gained access to an improved drinking water source over the period 1990-2008. Eastern Asia registered the largest gains in drinking water coverage—from 69 per cent in 1990 to 86 percent in 2008. Sub-Saharan Africa nearly doubled the number of people using an improved drinking water source—from 252 million in 1990 to 492 million in 2008.

Despite real progress, we are failing to reach the most vulnerable. Although many countries have demonstrated that progress is possible, efforts need to be intensified. They must also target the hardest to reach: the poorest of the poor and those disadvantaged because of their sex, age, ethnicity, or disability. Disparities in progress between urban and rural areas remain daunting.

- The poorest children have made the slowest progress in terms of improved nutrition

In 2009, nearly a quarter of children in the developing world were underweight, with the poorest children most affected. In Southern Asia, a shortage of quality food and poor feeding practices, combined with inadequate sanitation, has contributed to making underweight prevalence among children the highest in the world. In that region, between 1995 and 2009, no meaningful improvement was seen among children in the poorest households, while underweight prevalence among children from the richest 20 percent of households decreased by almost one third. Children living in rural areas of developing regions are twice as likely to be underweight as are their urban counterparts.

- Opportunities for full and productive employment remain particularly slim for women.

Wide gaps remain in women's access to paid work in at least half of all regions. Following significant job losses in 2008-2009, the growth in employment during the economic recovery in 2010, especially in the developing world, was lower for women than for men. Women employed in manufacturing industries were especially hard hit.

- Being poor, female or living in a conflict zone increases the probability that a child will be out of school. The net enrollment ratio of children in primary school has only gone up by 7 percentage points since 1999, reaching 89 percent in 2009. More recently, progress has actually slowed, dimming prospects for reaching the MDG target of universal primary education by 2015. Children from the poorest households, those living in rural areas and girls are the most likely to be out of school. Worldwide, among children of primary school age not enrolled in school, 42 percent—28 million—live in poor countries affected by conflict.

- Advances in sanitation often bypass the poor and those living in rural areas.

  Over 2.6 billion people still lack access to flush toilets or other forms of improved sanitation. And where progress has occurred, it has largely bypassed the poor. An analysis of trends over the period 1995-2008 for three countries in Southern Asia shows that improvements in sanitation disproportionately benefited the better off, while sanitation coverage for the poorest 40 percent of households hardly increased. Although gaps in sanitation coverage between urban and rural areas are narrowing, rural populations remain at a distinct disadvantage in a number of regions.

- Improving the lives of a growing number of urban poor remains a monumental challenge.

  Progress in ameliorating slum conditions has not been sufficient to offset the growth of informal settlements throughout the developing world. In developing regions, the number of urban residents living in slum conditions is now estimated at 828 million, compared to 657 million in 1990 and 767 million in 2000. Redoubled efforts will be needed to improve the lives of the urban poor in cities and metropolises across the developing world.

- Progress has been uneven in improving access to safe drinking water.

  In all regions, coverage in rural areas lags behind that of cities and towns. In sub-Saharan Africa, an urban dweller is 1.8 times more likely to use an improved drinking water source than a person living in a rural area.

Continued progress requires an active commitment to peace, equity, equality, and sustainability.

At the 2010 High-level Plenary Meeting of the General Assembly on the Millennium Development Goals, world leaders reaffirmed their commitment to the MDGs and called for intensified collective action and the expansion of successful approaches. They acknowledged the challenges posed by multiple crises, increasing inequalities, and persistent violent conflicts. They called for action to ensure equal access by women and girls to education, basic services, health care, economic opportunities and decision-making at all levels, recognizing that achievement of the MDGs depends largely on women's empowerment. World leaders also stressed that accelerated action on the goals requires economic growth that is sustainable, inclusive and equitable—growth that enables everyone to benefit from progress and share in economic opportunities.

Finally, further and faster movement toward achievement of the MDGs will require a rejuvenated global partnership, expeditious delivery on commitments already made, and an agile transition to a more environmentally sustainable future.

The Millennium Development Goals: Success and Failure

Goal 1: Eradicate extreme poverty and hunger
Target: Halve, between 1990 and 2015, the proportion of people who suffer from hunger. The proportion of people going hungry has plateaued at 16 percent, despite reductions in poverty.

Goal 2: Achieve primary universal education
Ensure that, by 2015, children everywhere, boys and girls alike, will be able to complete a full course of primary schooling. Sub-Saharan Africa has the best record for improvement in primary school enrolment.

Goal 3: Promote gender equality and empower women
Target: Eliminate gender disparity in primary and secondary education, preferably by 2005, and in all levels of education no later than 2015. Girls are gaining ground when it comes to education, though unequal access persists in many regions.

Goal 4: Reduce child mortality
Reduce by two thirds, between 1990 and 2015, the under-five mortality rate. Ten countries reduced their rates by at least half. Among them, Bangladesh, Eritrea, Lao People's Democratic Republic, Madagascar, Nepal and Timor-Leste recorded a 60 per cent drop or more.

Goal 5: Improve maternal health
Target: Reduce by three quarters, between 1990 and 2015, the maternal mortality ratio. Despite progress, pregnancy remains a major health risk for women in several regions.
Target: Despite proven interventions that could prevent disability or death during pregnancy and childbirth, maternal mortality remains a major burden in many developing countries.

Goal 6: Combat HIV/AIDS, malaria and other diseases

Target: Have halted by 2015 and begun to reverse the spread of HIV/ AIDS. New HIV infections are declining, led by sub- Saharan Africa, but trends in some other regions are worrisome.

* The incidence rate is the number of new HIV infections in a population over a certain period of time, expressed as a percentage of the adult population aged 15–49. For example, an incidence rate of 0.4 percent in sub-Saharan Africa in 2009 meant that 4 adults out of 1,000 were newly infected that year (leading to a total of 1.8 million new infections in the region). Between 2001 and 2009, the HIV incidence rate declined steadily, by nearly 25 per cent worldwide. However, this global progress masks substantial regional differences.

Goal 7: Ensure environmental sustainability

South America and Africa saw the largest net losses of forest areas between 2000 and 2010. Oceania also reported a net loss, largely due to severe drought and forest fires in Australia over the past decade. Asia, on the other hand, registered a net gain of some 2.2 million hectares annually in the past 10 years, mostly because of large-scale of forestation programs in China, India, and Vietnam. Rapid conversion of forested lands to other uses continued in many other countries in the region. The rich biodiversity of the world's forests remains imperiled by the still high rate of global deforestation and forest degradation as well as a decline in primary forests. One positive trend, however, is growth in the establishment of protected areas, which increased by 94 million hectares since 1990 and now cover an estimated 13 percent of the world's forests.

Goal 8: Develop a global partnership for development

Aid to developing countries is at a record high, but falls short of promises made in 2005. In 2010, net aid disbursements amounted to $128.7 billion, equivalent to 0.32 percent of developed countries' combined national income. This was the highest level of real aid ever recorded and an increase of 6.5 per cent in real terms over 2009. Tariffs on agricultural products from developing countries continue to fall, but remain unchanged for clothing and textiles.

Target: In cooperation with the private sector, make available the benefits of new technologies, especially information and communications. The world is increasingly interconnected through mobile, high-speed communications.

Index